Speaking the Truth in Love - Wins

A RESPONSE TO CHRISTIAN UNIVERSALISM

RON SEARS

JOURNEYMAN PRESS
ST. PETERSBURG, FLORIDA

Speaking the Truth in Love—Wins: A Response to Christian Universalism
Copyright © 2017 Ron Sears
All rights reserved.

Journeyman Press
St. Petersburg, Florida

ISBN-13: 978-1-947153-01-1
ISBN-10: 1-947153-01-3

www.journeymanpress.net
Cover Design: Eowyn Riggins
Interior Layout: Penoaks Publishing, http://penoaks.com

Thanksgiving...

I would like to offer thanks to David Stokes and his capable staff. This book would not have been printed without their tireless help. His encouragement to me in this project has been deeply appreciated.

I would also like to thank Tracey Dowdy. Her many hours of editing has (intended grammar for her) helped to produce the book in its current form.

I would also like to thank my "friend" for asking me to enter this journey. Though we have arrived at very different positions of faith, I continue to pray for him in his search for truth.

I would also like to thank the authors and leaders who have addressed the subject of Christian Hopeful Universalism (Trinitarianism). My heart and faith have been challenged and instructed by their efforts: Rob Bell, *Love Wins*; Francis Chan, *Erasing Hell: What God Said...*; Michael Brown, *Hyper-Grace, Exposing the Dangers*; Paul Ellis, *The Hyper-Grace Gospel, A Response*; David Anderson, *Free Grace Soteriology*; Malcolm Smith, *This Son of Mine: Discovering Your Identity*; Eric Metaxas, *Bonhoeffer: Pastor, Martyr, Prophet, Spy*; Tom Talbott; Kevin DeYoung; Charles Hodge, *Systematic Theology*; John Crowder, *Sons of Thunder*; Elmer Colyer, *Grace Communion International*; Alan Torrance, *Grace Communion International*; gci.org.

Dedication

I have developed this book as a study guide for the average reader. I have endeavored to show differing views of Christian Hopeful Universalism and the biblical basis for each – placing the thoughts as if you were sitting in a classroom listening to the author addressing the subject.

My prayer is that each reader is instructed by this information. I also pray the Holy Spirit will guide into His truth. The subjects of salvation, Heaven, and Hell, have eternal consequences and should be approached in prayer and a willingness to submit to the Holy Spirit and the truth He reveals in the Bible, God's Holy Word.

To God be the glory! – RS

Endorsements

"Dr. Sears takes a critical and sensitive topic regarding the justice and goodness of God and clearly presents differing perspectives. His commitment to biblical authority and proper hermeneutics leads any reader to consider these issues and discover truth. A very needed book for our day." —Eddie Lyons, President, Baptist Bible Fellowship International

"I am thankful for the detailed work and the heart with Ron Sears writes with. Ron addresses a very difficult topic with grace, compassion and sincere love for every reader. In a very detailed manner this book helps to understand the history, errors and results of Christian Universalism. Then Ron gives clear and accurate biblical insight to Scripture and its intended meaning. I am thankful for Ron and his effort." —Mark Milioni, President, Baptist Bible College, Springfield Missouri

"Historic Christian faith has always had some teachings that are more important than others. Ron Sears reminds us that what Jesus accomplished by His death and resurrection is most important. Christian Universalism trivializes the imperative of Jesus' death. It trivializes the consequences of rejecting God's grace. It is my hope that before people buy into this belief of unbelief, they will carefully read this book." —Dr. Mike Kalapp

"The Apostle Paul wrote to young pastor Timothy about the last days and how some would drift away from the faith because of 'seducing spirits.' No spirit is more seductive in our day and age than the tendency to water down important concepts like final judgment and even the idea of hell, itself. Ron Sears faces these issues head-on with this exhaustive study about the nature and danger of 'Christian Universalism.'" —David R. Stokes, Pastor and Wall Street Journal Best-Selling Author.

Table of Contents

Welcome to My Journey

This book has been written with the average reader in mind – it's how my mind functions. The following pages are a picture of the journey I have been on for quite some time. I would love to say I have *the* answers to this subject, but I cannot. However, I think I can say I have *some* answers, though I am still on my journey. I will leave the discerning of my answers up to you and the Holy Spirit working in your heart as you journey with me.

You may be wondering why anyone would write a book on this subject, and that is a fair question. The subject has been debated since the first centuries of Christianity. It has recently returned to the surface of spiritual thought and debate. As a result, I have done many hundreds of hours of study and research. What follows is a short expression of what I found. I entered this process with an open mind and a desire to know God's truth. I have reached the point in the process where I feel quite comfortable that, for me, I have found truth.

My road has had me learning biblical concepts that have been labeled by some as Trinitarian (Christian Hopeful Universalist) theology. As you read, some of the content will appear academic in nature. So, I am framing my thoughts as a response to questions you may have. Desiring this to be a common book for the reader, I do not go into many details of the original languages or contents that would cloud the understanding those of us who are not highly trained theologians or scholars (though chapters: Opinion of the Sages, and Textual

Consideration for "All" may require returning to a classroom setting), nor will I share information in a cranial manner. I will endeavor to list the information in a style that is easy to comprehend. My audience is you and my platform is for the general reader.

In process of writing, I have included and quoted from two papers (blogs). One, I feel and have been assured, fairly expresses the positions of those holding to Trinitarian Theology. The other is given in support of those who would take exception with Trinitarianism and hold to a more traditional view of the subject.

I hope to show what the overwhelming majority of scholars have held through the centuries. What I have found through my study is that history and the majority of theologians have held and continue to hold to the non-Trinitarian view. I will give a biblical basis for their view and allow the reader to discern for yourself the position you are led to hold. When dealing with the subject of biblical theology, merely being "new" (or old) is not a reliable test. Without irrefutable evidence to the contrary the continued reliance on the long held majority view espoused by individual scholars and the Christian church at large will always lead to a more secure understanding of doctrine.

I will also give extensive thoughts (quotes) from, Systematic Theology, written by Charles Hodge. These volumes are widely acceptance by many conservative and traditional theologians. It is a classic work of instruction on developing a consistent systematic approach to Biblical matters of doctrine. I have used his system and have found it reliable for determining biblical truth in my life. Perhaps it will do the same for you.

God is the Ultimate Author. He is the consummate Wordsmith. He has shared His thoughts with us in written word referred to as the Bible; God's Holy Word. Yet, it is a book that has been debated and caused disagreements among men as to its meaning. A sage once said, "Nothing can be said so clearly that it won't be misunderstood." The following pages are no exception.

I ask for charity in areas of question and would ask that you go to His Word to settle any controversy.

Throughout my writing I will, interchangeably, use the term Trinitarian with Christian Hopeful Universalism. I have not found much difference between the two terms. But, I have realized the term, Christian Hopeful Universalist, as the preferred description by those holding this doctrinal position.

My Conversation With A Trinitarian

(Christian Hopeful Universalist)

I am sharing a compilation of thoughts from my conversations with a Trinitarian (Christian Hopeful Universalist) friend. My journey began in earnest as a result of these talks. I have endeavored to be accurate in my statements and I have, to the best of my ability, shared the conversation as closely to quotations as I can.

I have condensed our talks to appear as one continuous communication. My words will be placed in "quotation marks" for ease of determining who is speaking. My friend's words will be placed in italics. Though not verbatim quotes, the restatements are as accurate as memory allows being taken from contemporaneous notes.

What I am sharing with you is new to me, but it is not a new belief. Church leaders have believed this since the first century after the Apostles. It was taught and written about by church fathers like Origen and others. My goal is to try to convert you to this thinking.

"But what did the majority of leaders believe? Didn't the early church take a stand against Origen and his beliefs?"

Everything you can ever see or know about God is found in Jesus. He is the expression of who and what God is like. All of God's attributes: His love, anger, mercy… To know what God is like, look at Jesus. God's wrath must be understood through the life of Jesus…

I cannot follow a god who is vindictive, punishing, or harsh. I find it very easy to follow a God of radical grace. It is comforting for me to speak with a parent who has lost a child and assure them that their child is safe because of God's radical grace. But it is hard for me to believe in a god who would send a 12 year old child (or whatever the age of accountability) to hell simply because he did not pray a prayer or exercise faith. I can however, with confidence tell that parent that their child is doing fine with this God of radical grace…

I'm not certain there is a literal hell. And if there is, I don't believe it has literal flame – how can you have fire and total darkness? What if Hell is the pain felt because of the separation from God? Or the pain caused by living in this world?

"How do you answer to Luke chapter 16? It seems to speak of a literal place with literal flames."

I feel that many of the stories in the Bible are allegories. The Old Testament has many stories without historical proof. They may have been placed in the Bible to teach a spiritual truth but may have been an allegory.

"What is hell to you?"

It is separation from God. It is possible that Heaven and Hell run together; they are the same place. The determination of whether it's Heaven or Hell is the person's relationship with God. If they are separated from God, the torment and knowledge of that separation may be what makes it Hell…

The pain one experiences on earth is Hell. Can you imagine a greater Hell than the pain and experience of things that some people endure?…

I believe that God will pursue everyone. He will continue to pursue them through eternity until they finally turn to Him.

"Does that mean that they will have a "second chance" after they die?"

Yes, I believe God will continually pursue them until they finally accept. So, they could have more than a second chance…

If you go to Heaven or Hell, you are there. If you choose to live in Hell, He's coming after you.

"Suppose they continue to reject this offer?"

I'm not certain about that…

"I am a 'Hopeful Universalist' – I have hope that every person, including Hitler, is in Heaven because Christ died for the sin of the whole world and by His faith we are forgiven. It is His faith not our faith. He has redeemed all; everyone.

"So, if you are consistent with this belief, then God would have to give Satan and his angels other chances too??"

Yes, I guess that's correct...

God's anger is not against us. His anger is dealing with what sin will do to us... God is not angry causing the Son to stand between us and Him protecting us from the Father's anger... I don't see the Old Testament books of the Law as revealing an angry God. They are there to point us to the grace of God's Son...

God does not love; He IS love...

I believe you (everyone) are a child of God's, whether you know it or not...

You do not have to exercise faith to be saved. I believe we are saved by the faith of Jesus. It is all of Him. He did it all for us and all we need to do is respond with a thank you (Gal 2:16; 2:20).

Our salvation is God's grace. He did it all on the cross. And our response is gratitude in what He's done...

"It would seem to me that your position is not any different than those who hold to the Calvinist belief. They believe only a select group are predetermined to be saved. While you believe everyone is predetermined to be saved."

I don't have an answer for that but I have never thought about that before...

When Paul preached on Mars Hill I believe the reason he could say those things was he was saying we are all God's children... (Acts 17:23-29)

"Speaking to you as a friend and accountability person I would suggest that you speak to your staff and board about these thoughts so that they are not informed at the same time as the general church membership."

I will think about that. But, I am going to handle this stealthily.

I don't think the Lord's Prayer is accurate for us today. If all of our sins are already forgiven, then how could Jesus say that the forgiveness of our sins is related to our forgiveness of others? Jesus was speaking to Old Testament saints in that prayer. Everything prior to the cross is Old Testament.

Do you believe that the Old Testament Jew had to have faith in the sacrifice offered on the Day of Atonement – or was it universally applied to all Jews?

"I'm not sure but I will check with a conservative Jewish friend of mine..."

(Several days later)… "I spoke with my friend and this was their response, 'On Yom Kippur (Day of Atonement) Jews were expected to make every effort to make amends with anyone they have offended BEFORE making the sacrifice. God is not responsible to forgive offenses between human beings and He will not consider forgiving someone who has not forgiven those who have offended him/her and who has made every attempt to seek forgiveness of someone they have offended. If the offended party refuses to forgive, then they are free to seek forgiveness of God for sins against God.

"'There are three levels of restitution: Personal, Society (your community) and the world.

"'Bottom line… The sacrifice is useless if the sinner is not willing to forgive or seek forgiveness….'

"I was also told, '…the Day of Atonement was effective only when joined by individual repentance. It was God's way of providing mercy to all who would receive it.'

"Do you believe all your sins are forgiven at birth?"

Yes.

"And so you believe when a person is born he is already a forgiven child of God?"

Yes, I do.

"Then you are a Universalist."

No. A universalist believes all roads lead to Heaven. I believe the only way to Heaven is through Jesus Christ. I believe someone can reject God's grace even in eternity.

"Would rejecting God's grace be a sin?"

Yes.

"Then you really don't believe all sins are already forgiven at birth."

No. I believe all sins are forgiven.

"Then you must admit you are a universalist..."

And this was the last time we spoke on the subject.

Rightly Dividing

It has been here for centuries – indications are that it began as an argument in the second century of church history. It has been debated; accepted; rejected; called fundamental to soteriology; and heresy. Ministers gathered a following and others have been removed because of their adherence to this subject. I have been told it is becoming the focal point of biblical truth in the world today; that it will truly change the face of the church moving forward into culture.

The name given to this theological subject is Trinitarianism. However, in current thought it is also referred to as Christian Hopeful Universalism. In my writing, both terms could be inserted for discussion. Immediately, the term, Trinitarian, raises the issue of the Trinity. Though the Trinity (belief in one God comprised of the Father, Son, and Holy Spirit) is connected to the discussion at some level, there is so much more. In some discussions, scholarly words are used causing many to turn to their dictionary for interpretation. If this doctrine was true, it would make life so much easier. It would remove the notion of the wrath of God entering your life. It would answer the questions of where a deceased loved one went; is there a hell; what about those living in a country devoid of the truth of God's love – and so much more.

If it were true, we could assure a parent that their teen who died from suicide is truly at peace in a better place. No longer would there be fear and pushback from the world towards a God who allows such things as poverty, mass death by a terrorist regime, the death of an innocent child, plagues, and any of the other calamities so often cited in these discussions.

In my discussions, I have been told that the difference between conservative historical Christianity and Trinitarianism is not more than "that much" (imagine holding your hand up with your index finger and thumb pointing parallel to each other while separated by less than ½ inch of space). I am expected to wonder if that ½ inch of separation is really that important.

In these talks, reading of books and pouring over the study materials, I must admit, the Trinitarian has some biblical basis for their position. At times, the verse(s) used can stand on their own as proof of the Trinitarian view. However, we are instructed to study the whole counsel of God. And as we do, we are encouraged to:

> *2 Timothy 4:1 I solemnly urge you in the presence of God and Christ Jesus, who will someday judge the living and the dead when he appears to set up his Kingdom: 2 Preach the word of God. Be prepared, whether the time is favorable or not. Patiently correct, rebuke, and encourage your people with good teaching.*
>
> *3 For a time is coming when people will no longer listen to sound and wholesome teaching. They will follow their own desires and will look for teachers who will tell them whatever their itching ears want to hear. 4 They will reject the truth and chase after myths.*
>
> *5 But you should keep a clear mind in every situation. Don't be afraid of suffering for the Lord. Work at telling others the Good News, and fully carry out the ministry God has given you. (NLT)*

I do not know if the world has entered a time when people will no longer "listen to sound and wholesome teaching," nor do

I have the ability to discern if we are "looking for teachers who will tell [us] whatever [our] itching ears want to hear." But I do know I want to "work at telling others the Good News, and fully carry out the ministry God has given" me.

In a recent discussion with an adherent of Trinitarian theology, we began speaking about where the authority for this position originates. I was assured that what he was telling me was based on the truth of God's Word and his desire to help me in my journey. So, as a sensei, he spoke to me about the necessity of rightly dividing God's Word. He further explained that, to him, this meant having a clear distinction made between the Old Covenant and the New. He also assured me that the New did not begin until after the death of Christ. He stated, "Most people, when they come to the end of the Old Testament, will turn to Matthew chapter one, and begin reading as if they are (wrongly) reading the words and truth of the New Covenant." He then quickly told me how wrong this was as he added, "The New Covenant was not in effect until the death of Christ."

"Christ was born under the law," he said. "He lived under the law. His preaching and teaching were under the law – the Lord's Prayer and the Sermon on the Mount are not for us today. They were for those living under the law."

As he continued, he said, "After Christ's death, everything became about grace. There is no more living under the law. We now live in the day of grace!"

The following is a continuation of that conversation. I am placing it here to help explain how the use of God's Word can result in right beliefs. However, it is also possible that the errant use of the Bible can develop the acceptance of error. It is left to us to discern if Trinitarianism is right or wrong. Is the belief in "radical / extreme grace" (which is an expanded belief of "Free Grace"), based on the truth of God's Word which has been rightly divided or not?

We continued our conversation - him speaking while I listened:

"Throughout the Old Testament it is always 'you… and me…' If you do this, then (God says) I will do this… It is a relationship between God and man. He says He has a part in the issue/action but assures us that we do too.

"In Jeremiah chapter 31, the process changes. God is pictured as doing all the action. It is **He** not **we** that is active. The reason for this change is produced in Christ after His death. The focus changes and it's all 'I'. God speaks and says 'I' will… Everything is all of Christ. And in the New Testament it is always, 'I' after the death of Christ. It's all about God and what He has done, is doing, and will do. The focus is entirely on Him not us.

"I believe we need to rightly divide the Bible" he said. "And I don't feel we do this today. We need to divide the Old Covenant from the New" (the old wine from the new wine, so to say – rs).

"Until His death, all of Christ's life, His teaching, and actions are part of the Old Testament law. Hebrews says it takes the death of the testator for the will to go into effect and it's the same with Christ. It took His death for the New Testament (covenant / will) to go into effect."

What do I do with this information? Am I to accept it because this person is a close friend? Do we readily accept teaching and doctrine because it sounds good or scratches our itching ears? Not at all.

In our conversation, he made reference to Paul's teaching to Timothy regarding rightly dividing God's Word. In fact, he used it as a foundation to help him arrive at his new understanding of God and His grace. He also used this verse as proof of the need for specific division of the Old and New Covenants. He went so far as to tell me that the only parts of biblical teaching that specifically apply to us today are those parts of Scripture after the cross.

In such matters, we need to become a detective. Nothing is accepted simply by face value alone. One must dig below the surface to find the meaning of the words and thoughts conveyed by the speaker / author. So, my first response is to look at the biblical meaning of the term "rightly dividing." How is it applied in understanding the word of God? Do those words mean predominantly (or only) the division between the Old and the New Covenant; or do they center more on accurately dividing the truth contained in any passage of Scripture or the whole counsel of God?

In the scripture referred to by my friend, Paul is teaching young Timothy. I searched the Bible and found his biblical reference in, 2 Timothy 2:15. Paul wrote to Timothy saying, "Study to shew thyself approved unto God, a workman that needeth not to be ashamed, rightly dividing the word of truth." (KJV is used because that is the version quoted by my friend)

I then looked to theologians who are recognized as fundamental and true in their shared opinions; those who have been acclaimed as experts in their understanding of the holy word. As I searched their writings, the following is what I found concerning Paul's meaning to Timothy in our text:

Treasury of Scripture Knowledge (a volume that examines Scripture by using Bible verses as proof text to other verses, becoming a book of the Bible on the Bible).

Verses listed related to "rightly dividing" in our text:

Matthew 13:44 "The Kingdom of Heaven is like a treasure that a man discovered hidden in a field. In his excitement, he hid it again and sold everything he owned to get enough money to buy the field. 45 "Again, the Kingdom of Heaven is like a merchant on the lookout for choice pearls. 46 When he discovered a pearl of great value, he sold everything he owned and bought it!

47 *"Again, the Kingdom of Heaven is like a fishing net that was thrown into the water and caught fish of every kind. 48 When the net was full, they dragged it up onto the shore, sat down, and sorted the good fish into crates, but threw the bad ones away. 49 That is the way it will be at the end of the world. The angels will come and separate the wicked people from the righteous, 51 throwing the wicked into the fiery furnace, where there will be weeping and gnashing of teeth. 51 Do you understand all these things?" "Yes," they said, "we do."*

52 *Then he added, "Every teacher of religious law who becomes a disciple in the Kingdom of Heaven is like a homeowner who brings from his storeroom new gems of truth as well as old." (NLT)*

Acts 20:20 I never shrank back from telling you what you needed to hear, either publicly or in your homes. 21 I have had one message for Jews and Greeks alike— the necessity of repenting from sin and turning to God, and of having faith in our Lord Jesus. (NLT)

Acts 20:26 I declare today that I have been faithful. If anyone suffers eternal death, it's not my fault, 27 for I didn't shrink from declaring all that God wants you to know. 28 "So guard yourselves and God's people. Feed and shepherd God's flock—his church, purchased with his own blood—over which the Holy Spirit has appointed you as elders. 29 I know that false teachers, like vicious wolves, will come in among you after I leave, not sparing the flock. 30 Even some men from your own group will rise up and distort the truth in order to draw a following. 31 Watch out! Remember the three years I was with you—my constant watch and care over you night and day, and my many tears for you.

32 *"And now I entrust you to God and the message of his grace that is able to build you up and give you an*

inheritance with all those he has set apart for himself. (NLT)

- **Adam Clarke Commentary:**

  > *The word orthotomein signifies:*
  > *1. Simply to cut straight, or to rectify.*
  > *2. To walk in the right way… walking in a right way [compared to] walking in a bad way. Thus to walk in a new way…*
  >
  > *Therefore, by rightly dividing the word of truth, we are to understand his continuing in the true doctrine, and teaching that to every person; and, according to our Lord's simile, giving each his portion of meat in due season-milk to babes, strong meat to the full grown, comfort to the disconsolate, reproof to the irregular and careless; in a word, finding out the necessities of his hearers, and preaching so as to meet those necessities.*

- **Barnes Notes:**

  > *The word here rendered 'rightly dividing,' occurs nowhere else in the New Testament. It means, properly, 'to cut straight, to divide right;' and the allusion here may be to a steward who makes a proper distribution to each one under his care of such things as his office and their necessities require; compare the notes at Matthew 13:52. Some have supposed that there is an allusion here to the Jewish priest, cutting or dividing the sacrifice into proper parts; others, that the allusion is to the scribes dividing the law into sections; others, to a carver distributing food to the guests at a feast. Robinson (Lexicon) renders it, 'rightly proceeding as to the word of truth;' that is, rightfully and skillfully teaching the word of truth. The idea seems to be,*

that the minister of the gospel is to make a proper distribution of that word, adapting his instructions to the circumstances and wants of his hearers, and giving to each that which will be fitted to nourish the soul for heaven.

- **Bible Knowledge Commentary:**

   The Greek orthotomounta, 'correctly handling,' found only here and in the Septuagint in Proverbs 3:6 and 11:5, means literally 'to cut straight,' but just what image Paul had in mind here is uncertain. Stone masons, plowers, road builders, tentmakers, and (least likely of all) surgeons have all been suggested, but a firm conclusion remains elusive. What is clear is that the shame of God's disapproval awaits those who mishandle His Word.

- **Bible Exposition Commentary:**

   The word study (2 Timothy 2:15) has nothing to do with books and teachers. It means 'to be diligent, be zealous.' It is translated in this way in 2 Timothy 4:9, 21, and also in Titus 3:12. The emphasis in this paragraph is that the workman needs to be diligent in His labors so that he will not be ashamed when his work is inspected. 'Rightly dividing' means 'cutting straight' and can be applied to many different tasks: plowing a straight furrow, cutting a straight board, sewing a straight seam.

   An approved workman knows that false doctrine is dangerous, and he will oppose it. Paul compared it to gangrene (2 Timothy 2:17). Much as gangrene spreads, infects, and kills other tissue, so false doctrine spreads and infects the body of believers, the church. This infection must be exposed and removed. Only the 'sound [healthy] doctrine' of the Word of God can keep a church healthy and growing.

- **Biblical Illustrator:**

The idea of rightness seems to be the dominant one; that of cutting quite secondary; so that the evaluations are quite justified in following the example of the Vulgate (recte tractantem), and translating simply 'rightly handling.' But this right handling may be understood as consisting in seeing that the word of truth moves in the right direction, and progresses in the congregation by a legitimate development.

I believe there is no preaching that God will ever accept but that which goes decidedly through the whole line of troth from end to end, and is always thorough, earnest, and downright. As truth is a straight line, so must our handling of the truth be straightforward and honest, without shifts or tricks.

Truth is of various kinds – physical, mathematical, moral, etc.; but here one particular kind of truth is referred to, called the word of truth – that is, the truth of the Word of God – the truth of Divine Revelation – theological truth. The Bible was not given to teach men philosophy, or the arts which have respect to this life; its object is to teach the true knowledge of God, and the true and only method of salvation.

1. The truths of God's Word must be carefully distinguished from error.

2. But it is necessary to divide the truth not only from error, but from philosophy, and mere human opinions and speculations.

3. The skillful workman must be able to distinguish between fundamental truths, and such as are not fundamental.

4. Rightly to divide the word of truth, we must arrange it in such order as that it may be most easily and effectually understood. In every system some things stand in the place of principles, on which the rest are built. He who would be a skillful workman in God's building must take much pains with the foundation; but he must not dwell forever on the first principles of the doctrine of Christ, but should endeavor to lead His people on to perfection in the knowledge of the truth.

5. A good workman will so divide the word of truth, as clearly to distinguish between the law and the gospel; between the covenant of works and the covenant of grace.

6. Another thing very necessary to a correct division of the word of truth is that the promises and threatenings contained in the Scriptures be applied to the characters to which they properly belong.

■ **Geneva Notes:**

By adding nothing to it, neither deleting anything, neither mangling it, nor rending it apart, nor distorting it: but marking diligently what his hearers are able to bear, and what is fit to edifying.

■ **Life Application Commentary:**

Because the term is used only here in the New Testament, we cannot be sure of its use, but the meaning is clear enough – approval of one's ministry before God will depend on how well one has proclaimed, explained, and applied the word of truth. We must help the gospel cut a straight path and do nothing to hinder it.

- **Matthew Henry:**

> *And what is their work? It is rightly to divide the word of truth. Not to invent a new gospel, but rightly to divide the gospel that is committed to their trust. To speak terror to those to whom terror belongs, comfort to whom comfort; to give everyone his portion in due season, Matthew 24:45. Observe here, 1. The word which ministers preach is the word of truth, for the author of it is the God of truth. 2. It requires great wisdom, study, and care, to divide this word of truth rightly; Timothy must study in order to do this well.*

Though there are a few comments given indicating it is dividing the law from grace, I believe it is evident the majority of scholars view Paul's teaching as dividing truth from error.

What is the importance of this nuance? One's position of "rightly dividing" will determine how they believe. If someone stands where my friend does, then the wrath of God poured out on humankind during the flood (because their actions were continually evil) cannot be applied to humanity today. Since the cross, all of God's wrath has been met (they say) in Christ. The mountains God refers to as Cursing and Blessing, which were given to Israel by God through Joshua, would no longer be conditionally applicable for us today. God would no longer say, "If you do this, then you can expect me to respond with that." There would only be the goodness of God's grace to look for today. Since the cross, God's grace is eternal and given to all. The Christian Hopeful Universalist holds there is no one who will be found outside the covenant of God's grace and blessing; it has been given to all men. The wrath of God has been met through

Christ and is no longer part of God's dealing with humanity individually or corporately.

These concepts are not trivial. They have eternal consequences. My prayer is that something shared in this book will open doors leading you to rightly divide God's truth for your life.

Enjoy your journey…

Systematic Theology

Charles Hodge

How can one study the Word of God, having confidence they are standing in His truth and understanding it as He intended? There must be a way; otherwise we are left to trust in what other people have said. If I want to be found standing in truth, and other spiritual people do as well, yet we end up on opposite sides of a subject, then someone must be wrong, correct?

Charles Hodge is the author of, Systematic Theology, a classic set of books designed to help a student of the Bible establish a system that rightly divides God's Word. His presentation is systematic and, if applied, will guide the student with steps for establishing what they believe. The result will be a more complete and accurate stance of doctrinal belief and positions held.

Dr. Hodge writes,

> *It may naturally be asked, why not take the truths as God has seen fit to reveal them, and thus save ourselves the trouble of showing their relation and harmony?*

That is a logical question. Why not allow truth to stand with little regard for how it interacts with other truth? Then there would not be a need for concern when one truth would collide with another.

Dr. Hodge answers his question by saying,

> *The answer to this question is, in the first place, that it cannot be done. Such is the constitution of the human mind that it cannot help endeavoring to systematize and reconcile that facts which it admits to be true... (ibid)*

Your mind will naturally place thoughts and held truth in an orderly system to discern their interaction and relationship with other held truth. And that order will be used when receiving new information. It will then compare that new information to your already held truth. That comparison will help you in discerning if the information should be embraced or dismissed.

As explained by Dr. Hodge, the importance of this is found, in our inability to know revealed truth and its relationship with other truth...

> *We cannot know what God has revealed in his Word unless we understand, at least in some good measure, the relation in which the separate truths therein contained stand to each other... (ibid)*

There are basically three main methods of discernment. It must be admitted that the names given these systems are not precise. Just like parables used in Scripture, one can find holes in consistency when moving in the realm of application. But, Dr. Hodge explains,

> *The methods which have been applied to the study of theology are too numerous to be separately considered. They may, perhaps, be reduced to three general classes: First, The Speculative; Second, The Mystical; Third, The Inductive. These terms are, indeed, far from being precise... (ibid)*

I will only look at the speculative and inductive methods. And to be fair, I will state that my choice of system is the inductive. I will also spend more time looking at the speculative than the inductive. It is my feeling that the objections to the speculative become self-evident. Therefore, a brief description of the inductive should be enough to define what is meant by the term and method.

The first system mentioned is that of speculation. In this system, it is assumed that what the mind determines to be true will be the filter for all new information received. It is therefore predetermined that information received is judged as true or false by what you already believe in your mind. Scripture is reconciled by reason rather than reason submitted to scripture. To this system rational evidence is the proof of biblical doctrine. Giving preference to apparent over realistic does harm to our moral nature. Faith is made submissive to what one knows (contrary to Hebrews 11:1,2). All events and information are then explained and defined by your held belief.

> *Speculation assumes… certain principles, and from them undertakes to determine what is and what must be. It decides on all truth, or determines on what is true from the laws of the mind, or from the axioms involved in the constitution of the thinking principle within us… (ibid)*

Dr. Hodge explains how this impacts our belief system as he writes,

> *Men lay down certain principles called axioms, or first truths of reason, and from them deduce the doctrine of religion by the course as rigid… This is sometimes done to the entire overthrow of the doctrines of the Bible… Conscience is not allowed to mutter in the presence of the lordly understanding… To this method the somewhat ambiguous term Dogmatism has been applied, because it attempts to reconcile the doctrines of Scripture with reason,*

and to rest their authority on rational evidence. The result of this method has always been to transmute, as far as it succeeded, faith into knowledge, and to attain this end the teachings of the Bible have been indefinitely modified. Men are expected to believe, not on the authority of God, but on that of reason. (ibid)

There must be a final authority for all held truth. The scientist looks to nature. The Christian (conservative) looks to the Bible which is believed to reveal the truth as God determines. As a result, the scientist should not interpret nature by his pre-held beliefs. Nature leads the man of science into believing the truth. As with developing a system of theology, the Bible reveals the accuracy of held opinions. The Bible is the test of belief – never the reverse. Confusion will result if we interpret the Bible through our philosophy.

The Bible is to the theologian what nature is to the man of science. It is his storehouse of facts; and his method of ascertaining what the Bible teaches... No man has a right to lay down his own opinions, however firmly held, and call them 'first truths of reason,' and make them the source or test of Christian doctrines... nothing which is not self-evident can be universally believed, and what is self-evident forces itself on the mind of every intelligent creature.

It may be admitted that the truths which the theologian has to reduce to a science, or, to speak more humbly, which he has to arrange and harmonize, are revealed partly in the external works of God, partly in the constitution of our nature, and partly in the religious experience of believers; yet lest we should err in our inferences from the works of God, we have a clearer evaluation of all that nature reveals, in his word; and lest we should misinterpret our own consciousness and the law of our nature, everything that can be legitimately learned from the source will be found recognized and authenticated in the Scriptures...

It is plain that complete havoc must be made of the whole system of revealed truth, unless we consent to derive our philosophy from the Bible, instead of explaining the Bible by our philosophy... It is a fundamental principle of all sciences, and of theology among the rest, that theory is to be determined by facts, and not facts by theory. (ibid)

We cannot assume a truth and then use that as a standard to understand the Bible. For a truth to be valid, it must be recognized in the Bible as true. For humanity to use our perceptions as foundational truth would lead to the development of as many belief systems as there are individuals.

All truth must be consistent. God cannot contradict himself. He cannot force us by the constitution of the nature which He has given us to believe one thing, and in his Word command us to believe opposite... All the truths taught by the constitution of our nature or by religious experience, are recognized and authenticated in the Scriptures. We cannot assume this or that principle to be intuitively true... and make them a standard to which the Bible must conform. What is self-evidently true, must be proved to be so, and is always recognized in the Bible as true. Whole systems of theologies are founded upon intuitions, so called, and if every man is at liberty to exalt his own intuitions, as men are accustomed to call their strong convictions, we should have as many theologies in the world as there are thinkers. (ibid)

Dr. Hodge declares that the best method of theological development is the inductive system. This method starts with the assumption that the Bible contains all the facts of theology. It also assumes that all theological facts contained in the scripture are consistent with each other. Then the natural progression would develop a consistent system of belief to form a doctrinal statement.

> *The true method of theology is, therefore, the inductive, which assumes that the Bible contains all the facts or truths which forms the contents of theology… also assumed that the relation of these Biblical facts to each other, the principles involved in them, the laws which determine them, are in the facts themselves, and are to be deduced from them, just as the laws of nature are deduced from the facts of nature. In neither case are the principles derived from the mind and imposed upon the facts, but equally in both departments, the principles or laws are deduced from the facts and recognized by the mind. (ibid)*

The commentaries I have studied and the books and opinion papers that most resonate with my heart and mind are those which have used this inductive method of systematic theology. Based on "these truths", they say, we can know "this" to be real (or false).

After intensive study, I would reject using the speculative approach to theology. In consideration of the Trinitarian (Christian Hopeful Universalism) theology, those using the speculative approach would, "…lay down certain principles called axioms, or first truths of reason, and from them deduce the doctrine of religion…" As a result, I believe this would necessarily lead them in the subject of grace. "…to the entire overthrow of the doctrines of the Bible…." relating to the Trinitarian approach to soteriology.

A snapshot of the position held by Trinitarians of Hell.

If incorrect, the Trinitarian view has repercussions, as Dr. Hodge wrote, "…to the entire overthrow of the doctrines of the Bible." Of course, I am sharing this statement as one who does not hold to the Christian Hopeful Universalist doctrine. I am certain it sounds harsh and wholly inaccurate by those who do; especially my friend. As such, allow me to soften Dr. Hodge's words by saying, the Trinitarian view has altered some doctrines held by the majority of historical Christian doctrinal positions and scholars.

It would be logical to wonder if it matters which side of this question one accepts. So let me ask, does it matter what one believes about the doctrines of Heaven; Hell; God's wrath; whether God eternally pursues humanity; is there an end to accepting His grace; is one born again as a result of the faith of Christ alone; and are we given opportunity to respond to God's grace after death? What are the ramifications of God's reconciliation and forgiveness? Is it universal? If it is, does it apply universally to all humans?

I could go on but I think you get the picture. There is no way I can adequately give a detailed exposition on these subjects. Instead, allow me to highlight a few. If I uncover questionable doctrine, then perhaps Trinitarianism (Christian Hopeful Universalism) should be avoided altogether.

If one should follow the systematic structure given by Dr. Hodge… The true method of theology is, therefore, the inductive, which assumes that the Bible contains all the facts or truths which forms the contents of theology… also assumed that the relation of these Biblical facts to each other… are to be deduced from them… In neither case are the principles derived from the mind and imposed upon on the facts, but equally in both departments, the principles or laws are deduced from the facts and recognized by the mind.

... then it is not the mind that imposes upon the facts, but rather the principles or laws deduced from the facts which are recognized by the mind. Never allow what seems to be, to determine what truly is; do not use what the mind and soul would like, to dictate what God declares to be true.

I think it is important to understand the Trinitarian (Christian Hopeful Universalist) view as described by those holding this view. It seems all (most) Christian Hopeful Universalist question the existence of Hell. Is it a literal place of fire and punishment; is it everlasting; can one be saved from the penalty of sin once he has entered eternity? To help explain their belief, I have included the thoughts of a few learned men who hold the Trinitarian view.

In their own words what do Trinitarian Universalists believe about hell?

- **John Crowder:**

    For instance, there are a plethora of verses on hell and eternal torment. But there is also a plethora of verses on universal salvation for all mankind. Which of these verses do you throw away? Be careful taking scissors to your Bible in any direction! Rather than drawing hard lines of debate, Trinitarian theology holds these things in the tension of paradox, keeping hope for mankind without jumping into dogmatic assumptions. We must look at all sides of scripture to arrive at honest answers. But there are places where your logic (even your best theo-logic) will not provide answers."

- ## Keith Stump: The Battle Over Hell

It took the Christian community hundreds of years to come up with a consensus on the issue (of a literal hell — rs). The majority view — that hell is a place of eternal fiery torment — emerged only after a long debate within the Church. While most Christians agree that the essence of hell is alienation from God, the in-house debate is over the specifics — where hell is, when it is, how hot it is and how long it is.

Why? Because the Bible offers little detail. Hell is a doctrine about which there is no clear and dogmatic teaching in Scripture. The interpretation of biblical statements and the imagery they employ is beset with difficulties.

As hell appears to be a harsh doctrine, many Christians today choose to explain it in ways that soften its impact. The modern trend has been to replace the traditional fire-and-brimstone concept of hell as a place of eternal torture with a more politically correct portrayal of hell as a condition of spiritual anguish caused by alienation from God. In other words, hell is not a place but a state.

- ## Elmer Colyer, Grace Communion International

(Notes taken from a free video and study notes download found on the web site of Grace Communion International)

We don't want to get rid of the wrath of God but it must be united in a seamless way with His love.

There are two God's (in Christianity – rs); God of wrath and a God of love. They aren't reconciled.

How does hell fit into the picture of hell and God's love? Where do we finally see the holiness and wrath and judgment of God against sin finally finding its proper place? It's on the cross. In Revelation chapter 5 you have the Lion of Judah and the Lamb of God slain. There's no difference. The final revelation is what took place on the cross. So this means that whatever punishment occurs in hell cannot be the same as Christ endured on the cross. It can only bear witness to that fact.

The cross revealed the wrath of God against sin and the love of God for sinners. So God loves the sinners in hell. So we have to not only relate hell to the judgment that takes place but also the love of God.

What if hell is a better place for sinners who in their folly reject the love of God in Christ and Heaven? Isaiah 6, 'Woe is me for I am undone...' What if hell isn't simply a place of punishment? What if it's a place of refuge where the sinner is shielded from the unmediated presence of God because they finally turned away from Christ? ... 'Hell is a refuge if it hides me from your frown.' (A quote from the deathbed of an infidel).

So we relate hell to the love of God and it becomes a refuge for the sinner and his or her unrepentance is shielded from the very presence of God...

Hell points back to the cross and that takes seriously the sin, brokenness and evil in this world. And deals with it objectively."

- **Joseph Tkach**

> *Humans don't have a good handle on justice or mercy. Humans aren't qualified to judge such matters of eternal consequence.*
>
> *If we take Jesus seriously when he teaches about mercy, we should take him seriously when he teaches about punishment.*
>
> *Mercy only has meaning if we are escaping a real punishment."*

- **Alan Torrance, Grace Communion International (wrath of God and Hell)**

(free download from Grace Communion International web site)

> *When we are speaking of the wrath of God, we are speaking of the love of God. There are two kinds of anger – wrath that emerges when someone's will is frustrated (as your team loses and you get angry). A lot of people see God's wrath this way. But that is an unbiblical view. The wrath of God is the wrath of a jealous God... God's wrath, God's jealousy, is God's love for his people. The wrath of God is God's anger at the cost of sin.*
>
> *What is hell? (question asked by the interviewer)?*
>
> *Hell is a place of separation from God. Godlessness.*
>
> *Do you mean separation in the sense of alienation or space (question by interviewer)?*
>
> *Alienation. People standing against God; trying to live without God.*
>
> *The kingdom of God... one day the kingdom will be fully realized. But the kingdom is now at hand. Just as... we have to say the same about hell. To the sense we try to stand against God and live without God, hell is already realized in some sense.*

What we can say about the population of hell. First, to the extent that hell is populated it's populated by people who are loved by God. Second, to the extent that hell is populated it's populated by people for whom Christ died and who Christ has forgiven. Just as we are to forgive 70 times 7... Jesus wouldn't ask us to do something he wouldn't do himself. To the extent that hell is populated it is populated by those God has allowed to opt to live against his purpose. And if that happens and to the extent hell is populated, God is utterly distraught for eternity... Finally, it is not possible to be a Christian and want hell to be populated. Why? Because we are to love our enemies. That means all our enemies...

When it comes to the future destination of people... we say this, The only God we know is God whose all-loving and is all-just, and all-forgiving, who'd never do anything that is contrary to his love, his justice, and forgiveness. Therefore, we can joyfully commit those people to God... given that God loves them more than even we do... Because he descended to hell for us....

- **Thomas Talbott**

Hell, as described in the Bible, exists

It is partially here as the Kingdom of Darkness that all men are born into.

It will be fully present for those who persist in rejecting God's gift of salvation. However, God's grace and gift of faith reaches everyone while they are dead in their sins (Ephesians 2:1, Colossians 2:13) and there is no biblical text that says his mercy and gift of salvation will end when one dies physically. Jesus Christ is proclaimed to be the Lord of the dead and the living (Romans 14:9).

Hell is not retribution but rehabilitation

The suffering in hell is the anguish of a soul persisting in rebellion against God, or the shame of a soul when it realizes how much it has sinned against a holy God as well as profound regret for what might have been.

There are three (3) generally accepted understandings of hell:

1. *A literal place of fire where the damned suffer eternal conscious torment.*
2. *A metaphorical hell where the suffering is real but is not literally fire and brimstone. The pain may be physical, emotional or spiritual.*
3. *Conditional, where souls are punished until retributive justice is met or accomplished, after which these punished souls are annihilated*

In their own words, what Trinitarians believe about salvation

- **Grace Communion International**

All humanity was included in the results of the first Adam, and all humanity is included in the results of the second Adam, Jesus. It's not just a few people that God chose ahead of time, and it's not just one particular nation, or one particular social class – God's plan is for everyone he has created – and that means everyone. Jesus really is Lord of all.

Adam messed it up, but Jesus did it right—and in Christ, all humanity has a fresh start on being 'the image of God.' Jesus is the key to our transformation – not only is he the model that we copy, but he is also the engine that drives the whole process. He supplies the power and the direction.

- **Wikipedia (I understand this is not considered the most credible source. However, I am including it to reflect the contemporary view held by a secular source.)**

  Traditionally, the doctrine of Universalism was traced by Universalist historians back to the teachings of Origen of Alexandria (c.185–284), an influential early Church Father and writer. Origen believed in apocatastasis, the ultimate restoration and reconciliation of creation with God, which was interpreted by Universalists historians to mean the salvation and reconciliation with God of all souls which had ever existed, including Satan and his demons. However more recent research has shown that this analysis of Origen's views is uncertain. Origen also believed in the pre-existence of souls and that glorified Man may have to go through cycles of sin and redemption before reaching perfection. The teachings of Origen were declared anathema at the Ecumenical Council of 553, centuries after his death, though Gregory of Nyssa, another figure to whom Universalist historians attributed Universalist belief, was commended as an Orthodox defender of the faith by the same Council. Universalist historians have also identified Johannes Scotus Eriugena (815–877) and Amalric of Bena (c. 1200) as Universalists. Much of this research was incorporated by French priest Pierre Batiffol into an article on Apocatastasis later translated for the 1911 Catholic Encyclopedia.

- ## Thomas Talbott

Thomas Talbott offers three propositions which are biblically based, but which he asserts to be mutually exclusive:

1. *God is omnipotent and exercises sovereign control over all aspects of human life and history.*
2. *God is omni-benevolent, is ontologically Love, and desires the salvation of all people.*
3. *Some (many) persons will experience everlasting, conscious torment in a place of (either literal or metaphorical) fire.*

Traditional theology clarifies omnipotence or omni-benevolence to resolve the contradiction. Calvinism resolves it by positing a doctrine of limited atonement, which claims that God's love is restricted. Only a select number of people are elected to be saved, which includes redemption and purification. This demonstrates a special love, and most people (the 'eternally reprobate' or non-elect) are given only common grace and tolerance. This bifurcation of grace intends to retain a doctrine of God's omni-benevolence and a doctrine of hell. In comparison, Arminianism resolves the contradiction by rejecting divine omnipotence with respect to human will. This is commonly referred to as synergism. It posits that human beings have an inviolable free will, which allows the choice of accepting or rejecting God's grace. Universalists disagree with the third claim, and argue that all people receive salvation.

Since traditional interpretations of multiple biblical verses seem to be about people experiencing everlasting conscious torment in hell, many Christians hold that Universalists must either refute or reinterpret these verses. There are many verses of scripture supporting universal salvation with which supporters of eternal damnation must contend, including (but not limited to): Matthew 18:14, Luke 3:6, John 3:17, John 12:32, John 12:47, John 15:16, Romans 8:38-9, 1 Timothy 2:3–4, and 1 Timothy 4:9–10.

- *God is Trinity*

God is One Being and Three Persons, Father, Son and Holy Spirit, who indwell each other in a perichoretic communion of love.

- *God is Love*

God is ontologically love (1 John 4:8), and everything that he is and does reflect his being love. His holiness is an aspect of His love and can be thought of as one thing: Holy lovingkindness.

- *Reconciliation is through Christ Jesus*

Jesus Christ is the incarnation of the Second Person of the Trinity and he is both fully God and fully man. Because he created everything and everything inheres in him, all of creation was crucified and resurrected with him. (John 1:3–4), (Colossians 1:15–20). Because divinity and humanity meets in him, mankind are now participants in the perichoresis or the divine dance of love within the Trinity.

- *Universal atonement of sins*

Jesus Christ's death on the cross paid the price for the sins of the world (Romans 5:15–19) and all men are reconciled to God (2 Corinthians. 5:19). No human being is alienated from God as he is their only source of life (John 1:3–4) and in him they live and move and have their being. (Acts 17:28)

Because all sins have been paid for, all sins are forgiven. Divine forgiveness precedes human response and this forgiveness is both love and judgment because to say, 'I forgive you' is to say 'I love you' and 'You have sinned against me'. Man can respond by agreeing with the judgment (repentance) and receive both the love and forgiveness or he can deny the judgment and refuse God's love and forgiveness.

- *Salvation is an objective reality and a subjective reality*

A personal response of faith is required before the objective saving act of God is made subjectively real in the individual's life. The response is transformative and changes with knowledge and experience. What has been accomplished for all mankind must be accomplished in each person's life which requires the individual's cooperation with the Holy Spirit. God is love and man is loved but he must be in relationship with him to know that love. It is the difference between being and knowing.

- *The Good News is about the Kingdom of God*

The mission is not just to save people from hell but to bring them out of the Kingdom of Darkness and into the Kingdom of Light. All moral law can be summed up by the two Great Commandments: Love God and Love Others (Romans 13:8–10) and these two commands are not distinct and exclusive. To love God is to love others and to love others is to love God.

- *The Kingdom of God is here and yet not fully here*

Trinitarian Universalists live in that dialetic tension and in the hope of the future Kingdom. (1 Corinthians. 13:12)

- *Wrath and judgment is another face of Love*

God's love is passionate and people can grieve him (Ephesians 4:30) by thwarting his love and good intentions toward them. If man hurts himself or others, he will experience that divine love as wrath. Judgment accompanies wrath and judgment is salvific. It is a fire that purifies and refines, not one that destroys. (Malachi 3:2) If man is not judged and if he does not feel God's wrath, he will not be aware that he has sinned. Judgment and wrath encourages a man to stop what he is doing and repent (turn around). Then he will know forgiveness and feel God's love turn from wrath to warmth.[21]

- *True justice is restoration and reconciliation*
- *Justice is not fully met by punishing wrongdoers. True justice is*
- *restoration of what was stolen or destroyed*
- *repentance and reformation of the sinner*
- *reconciliation between the sinner and God and the person(s) sinned against*
- *The final word God speaks to Mankind is always reconciliation and redemption*

Sodom is portrayed as a very wicked place that was judged by God and destroyed by burning sulfur (Genesis 19:1–29). Jude writes that they 'suffered the punishment of eternal fire' (Jude 1:7). But Jesus knew what circumstances would have brought the people of Sodom to repentance and acknowledgement of God (Matthew. 11:23). The last word God speaks over Sodom is restoration in an eschatological prophecy by Ezekiel (Ezekiel 16:53–55).

Universalists believe that every person will be saved, where more orthodox Roman Catholics believe that only those who died in God's grace will find purgation for their venial sins in Purgatory.

The Argument

There are four (4) major theories about human salvation in Christendom:

1. *Exclusivism: Salvation is exclusively found in Christianity. Anyone who is not a Christian will go to hell.*

2. *Inclusivism: Some adherents of other religions may find salvation, but it is still only Jesus Christ who can (and may or will) save them.*

3. *Pluralism: One's own religion is not the sole and exclusive source of truth; salvation, in principle, may be found in any religion, although salvation is not necessarily found in one's search of any (other) religion(s).*

4. *Universalism: All persons (and peoples?) will be saved.*

Christian denominations and churches will generally profess one of the above to be true and the others as error; however, they are not all mutually exclusive. For example, some who hold to #4 'Universalism' also hold to #1 'Exclusivism.' For these, anyone who is not a Christian will go to hell, but ultimately everyone will become a Christian and therefore be saved. Others may be #2 'Inclusivists' and #3 'Pluralists.' For those who might hold to these, because God may use the tools of any particular religion or culture to reveal his grace in Christ (Inclusivism), other religions therefore, potentially exhibiting the effects of this work, may in fact hold valuable insights to truth for theology (Pluralism), consequently calling the members of a particular congregation/denomination/religion to be open to that possibility.

Questions and Answers About Trinitarian Theology

Grace Communion International

(shared from printable article found on the Grace Communion International web site)

- **Let's address several questions and objections. Q. Are you saying there is no difference between a Christian and a non-Christian?**

A. No. We are saying that because of who Jesus is and what he has done, all humans—believers and non-believers—are joined to God in and through Jesus, through his human nature. As a result, God is reconciled to all people, all have been adopted as his dearly loved children. All, in and through Jesus, are included in the Triune love and life of God: Father, Son and Spirit.

However, not all people acknowledge who Christ is and therefore the truth of who they are in Christ. They have not yet put repented and put their trust exclusively in Christ, are not believers. They are not personally living in relationship with him and receiving the abundant life he gives.

One way to speak of the distinction between believers and non-believers is to say that all people are included in Christ (objectively) but only believers actively participate (personally) in that inclusion.

We see these distinctions spoken of throughout the New Testament, and they are important. However, we must not take these distinctions too far, creating some kind of separation or opposition, and think of non-believers as not accepted by and not loved by God. To see them in this way would be to overlook the great truth of who Jesus Christ is and what he has done already for all humanity. It would be to turn the 'good news' into 'bad news.'

When we see all humanity joined to Christ, some of the categories we might have held in our thinking fall away. We no longer see non-believers as 'outsiders' but as children of God in need of personally acknowledging how much their Father loves them, likes them, and wants them. We approach them as brothers and sisters. Do they know who they are in Christ? Do they live in personal communion with Christ, No—and it is our privilege to tell them of God's love for them that they might do so.

- **Q. If all are reconciled already to God in Christ, why does Scripture say so much about repentance and faith?**

A. In the New Testament, the Greek word translated 'repentance' is *metanoia,* which means 'change of mind.' All humanity is invited and enabled by the Spirit to experience a radical change of mind away from sinful egoistic self-centeredness and toward God and his love experienced in union with Jesus Christ through the Holy Spirit.

Notice Peter's invitation to this change of mind in Acts 2:38-39: 'Repent and be baptized, every one of you, in the name of Jesus Christ for the forgiveness of your sins. And you will receive the gift of the Holy Spirit. The promise is for you and your children and for all who are far off—for all whom the Lord our God will call.'

God does not forgive people in exchange for their repentance and belief. As Scripture proclaims, forgiveness is an unconditional free gift that is entirely of grace. It is a reality that exists for us even before we enter into it in our experience. We repent because we are forgiven.

The gospel truth—the truth about Jesus and about all humanity joined with God in Jesus—is that God has already forgiven all humanity with a forgiveness that is unconditional and therefore truly free: 'Therefore,' invites Peter, 'repent and believe this truth—and be baptized by the Spirit with the mind of Jesus—which involves supernatural assurance that we truly are the children of God.'

Repentance is a change of mind and heart; it involves coming to acknowledge who Jesus is for us and who we are in him, apart from anything we have done or will yet do. Through repentance, which is God's gift to us through the Spirit, our minds are renewed in Jesus and we turn to him and begin to trust him.

The Spirit moves us to repent because our forgiveness has already been accomplished in Christ, not in order to be forgiven. We repent because we know that, in Jesus, our sins have already been forgiven, and that, in Jesus, we are already a new creation. In this repentance, we turn away from the alienation within us as the Spirit baptizes our minds in Jesus' acceptance and in the assurance that comes with it.

- **Q. Why does Paul say that if you don't have the Spirit, you don't belong to Christ?**

A. Romans 8:9 says, 'You, however, are not in the realm of the flesh but are in the realm of the Spirit, if indeed the Spirit of God lives in you. And if anyone does not have the Spirit of Christ, they do not belong to Christ.'

The sentence 'And if anyone does not have the Spirit of Christ, they do not belong to Christ' is not meant to be lifted out of context and turned into a proof that some people do not belong to God. In the context of this passage, Paul is addressing believers; he is not making a statement here about non-believers. He is warning disobedient believers who are refusing to submit to the Holy Spirit in their lives. In effect, he is saying, 'You say that the Spirit of God is in you, and you are right. However, your life should be reflecting the presence of the Spirit of Christ. Your actions do not demonstrate that you really do belong to Christ as you claim to. I don't dispute that. But if you do, then on that very basis act in accordance with that reality.'

As Paul says to believers in verse 12, 'We have an obligation—but it is not to the flesh…' (see verses 10-17).

▪ Q. If the world is reconciled, why would Jesus say that he doesn't pray for the world?

A. In John 17:9, Jesus says: 'I pray for them [his disciples]. I am not praying for the world, but for those you have given me, for they are yours.'

Just because Jesus said in one instance that he was not praying for the world, but instead for his disciples, does not imply that he never prayed for the world. It is just that right then, his emphasis was on his disciples. He is praying in particular for them, focusing on them.

It is also important to understand how John uses the word 'world' (kosmos in Greek) in the flow of his Gospel. At times the word can refer to all people (who are all loved by God; see John 3:16 while at other times it can refer to the worldly 'system' that is fallen and hostile toward God.

It is apparently this system that Jesus has in mind in John 17. Since this fallen system or world resists God, Jesus' prayer does not include it. He is not praying for the world in its current fallen form, rather, he is praying for a group of people whom he can use to declare his love in this fallen world.

Later on in his prayer, Jesus does turn his attention specifically to those who are not yet his disciples. He prays 'also for those who will believe in me through their message.' And what he prays for them is that they, along with those who are already believing, 'may be one, Father...so that the world may believe that you have sent me' (John 17:21). This aligns with the Gospel of John's message (3:16): God loves the whole world and wants to save everyone.

- **Q. If all are reconciled already to God, why does Scripture speak of hell?**

A. Scripture speaks of hell because it is the natural consequence of rebellion against God. When we cut ourselves off from God and refuse his mercy, grace and forgiveness we are rejecting communion with him and cutting ourselves off from the very source of our life. Christ came to prevent that from happening. Grace enters in and disrupts the natural course of a fallen creation. Being created for personal communion with means we must be receptive to what he has done for us in Christ. All are included in what Christ intends for everyone, but we can refuse our inclusion. We are reconciled to the Father, but we can refuse that to receive that reconciliation and live as if God had not reconciled us to himself.

However, such refusal does not negate what God has done for all humanity in Christ.

In *The Great Divorce,* C.S. Lewis wrote:

"There are only two kinds of people in the end; those who say to God, 'Thy will be done,' and those to whom God says, in the end, 'Thy will be done.' All that are in hell, choose it. Without that self-choice there could be no hell. No soul that seriously and constantly desires joy will ever miss it. Those who seek find. To those who knock it is opened."

- **Q. Why does the Bible talk about people whose names are not in the book of life?**

A. Revelation 13:8 says, 'All inhabitants of the earth will worship the beast—all whose names have not been written in the Lamb's book of life, the Lamb who was slain from the creation of the world.'

Revelation 17:8 says, 'The inhabitants of the earth whose names have not been written in the book of life from the creation of the world will be astonished when they see the beast.'

We need to consider the literary context of these statements in Revelations. John writes using a literary genre (style) known as apocalyptic. This genre, which was commonly used by Jewish writers in John's day, is highly symbolic. There is not a literal 'book of life.' The 'book of life' is a figure of speech, a symbolic way of referring to those who are in allegiance with the Lamb. These verses in Revelations refer to people who reject the new life that Christ has already secured for them.

- **Q. Why does Peter say it is hard to be saved?**

A. 1 Peter 4:17-18 says: 'For it is tie for judgment to begin with God's household; and if it begins with us, what will the outcome be for those who do not obey the gospel of God? And, 'If it is hard for the righteous to be saved, what will become of the ungodly and the sinner?'

The point of verses 17-18 is found in verse 19: 'So then, those who suffer according to God's will should commit themselves to their faithful Creator and continue to do good.'

Peter has been encouraging persecuted believers to live in accord with their identity as children of God and not like those who live in debauchery and idolatry (verses 1-5). The difficulty is not in Jesus' power to save but for those believing to live faithfully through times of the suffering of persecution. The difficulties involved in being saved call for perseverance. And in any case Peter does not say that salvation is impossible for anyone. (See also Mark 10:25-27), where Jesus replies to his disciples query as to how anyone could be saved if it was difficult for the wealthy. Jesus answered, 'For mortals it is impossible, but not for God; for God all things are possible,' NRSV).

As part of his argument, he points out that persecution is participation in the suffering of Christ, and therefore if believers are to suffer, they should suffer for their faith and godly behavior instead of suffering for sinful and ungodly behavior (verses 12-16). His point is that believers, who know that Jesus, the Savior, is the merciful Judge of all, should not be living in the same base and evil ways as those who oppose Christ even under the threat of persecution.

It is actually impossible for anyone to be saved—were it not for Christ. Christ has done what is impossible for humans to do for themselves. But those who reject Christ are not participating in Christ's suffering; they participate in their own suffering as they reap what they sow. And that experience is a far more difficult path to be on than the narrow one of those who know Christ and can have fellowship with him even in their sufferings.

- **Q. What is everlasting contempt and destruction?**

A. Daniel 12:2 reads, 'Multitudes who sleep in the dust of the earth will awake: some to everlasting life, others to shame and everlasting contempt.'

2 Thessalonians 1:6-9 says, 'God is just: He will pay back trouble to those who trouble you and give relief to you who are troubled, and to us as well. This will happen when the Lord Jesus is revealed from heaven in blazing fire with his powerful angels. He will punish those who do not know God and do not obey the gospel of our Lord Jesus. They will be punished with everlasting

destruction and shut out from the presence of the Lord and from the glory of his might.'

Both of these passages refer to the time of the final judgment when Jesus is 'revealed' (sometimes referred to as the Second Coming or Jesus' 'return in glory'). This is the time when all humans will see clearly who Jesus is and thus who they are because of who he is and what he has done. And this 'revelation' presents to them a choice—will they say 'yes' to their belonging to Christ, or will they say 'no'?

Their decision neither creates nor destroys their inclusion, but it does determine their attitude toward it—whether they will accept God's love for them and enter the joy of the Lord, or continue in alienation and frustration (and thus in shame and everlasting contempt and destruction) The destruction is a self-destruction as they refuse the purpose for which they have been made, and the redemption that has already been given to them. They refuse to submit to God's righteousness through repentance and so refuse to receive his life, thereby effectively cutting themselves off from it.

In the Judgment, everyone will face Jesus, the Judge who died for all, and they will have to decide whether they will trust him and count on his being judged in their place. Those who trust their Savior agree with the judgment of God as to what is evil and must be done away with. They humbly receive the joy of the life God has given them in Christ. Those who reject him continue in their hostility and the hell that goes with their living in denial of the truth and of reality of their sin and of Christ's salvation for them.

- ■ **Q. What about the 'narrow gate'?**

A. Jesus says in Matthew 7:13-14: 'Enter through the narrow gate. For wide is the gate and broad is the road that leads to destruction, and many enter through it. But small is the gate and narrow the road that leads to life, and only a few find it.'

Jesus describing what is happing in the present. A clearer translation is: 'many are entering' and 'only a few are finding it.' In his day, at that time, most were living on the 'broad road' of destruction. What Jesus offers here is descriptive not prescriptive. It does not say what Jesus wants nor what God intends. In fact, this is a warning and warnings are given to reveal the negative outcome from occurring. No parent says to their child, 'Watch out, a car is coming!' because they hope the child gets run over! And Jesus gives the reason for the need to be warned: under fallen conditions the way to destruction is wide, inviting and easy to follow, or we can simply be swept along into it. The narrow way to life can be easy to miss, may seem difficult to follow and takes our being deliberate and intentional. There were only a 'few' who had at that time embraced the truth that is in Jesus—and it is he who is 'the narrow gate.' But Jesus wants to turn that around so that there are many, not a few, who enter into the life that Jesus has for them. So he gives this warning out of his love for them.

Jesus addresses a similar issue in Matthew 7:21-23: 'Not everyone who says to me, 'Lord, Lord,' will enter the kingdom of heaven, but only the one who does the will of my Father who is in heaven. Many will say to me on that day, 'Lord, Lord, did we not prophesy in your name, and in your name drive out demons and in your name perform many miracles?' Then I will tell them plainly, 'I never knew you. Away from me, you evildoers!'

These people have done miracles, and in doing so have deceived many. They claim to know Jesus. Although Jesus obviously knows them (he is omniscient), he does not see himself in them with regard to their actual faith or behavior, and so he proclaims, 'I never knew you.' That is, I don't recognize you as a follower of mine. We haven't been in relationship, in communion, with one another despite what you were doing.

■ **Q. But don't we become God's children only at the point of belief?**

A. 'Yet to all who did receive him, to those who believed in his name, he gave the right to become children of God—children born neither of natural descent, nor of human decision or a husband's will, but born of God.'

We have already seen in Scripture that God has provided for everyone in the vicarious humanity of Jesus. When he died, we all died; when he rose, we rose. Our human natures have been regenerated in him. Therefore all humans are, from God's perspective, already adopted into his family. In Jesus, God gives people that 'right' long before they accept it and live in it. They have an inheritance, as Paul puts it.

If we say that we don't have a right to become the children of God until after and unless we believe, then we end up denying what John goes on to say: that it doesn't come from natural descent or from human decision. Such an understanding would make our having the right be dependent upon our decision!

Those who believe in and accept Jesus as their Lord and elder brother, enter into and begin to experience the new life as children of God. But that place in God's family has been theirs all along, the new life that has been 'hidden with Christ in God'. In other words, what has been objectively true for them all along in Jesus, becomes subjectively and personally experienced by them when they become believers. They begin taking up their right and living as the children of God.

■ **Q. Is this universalism?**

A. No, not in the sense that every person ultimately will be saved (or enter into or receive their salvation) regardless of whether they ever trust in Christ. There is no salvation outside of Jesus Christ (Acts 4:12). Those who somehow absolutely refuse to enter into their salvation, receive it by repentance and faith in what Christ their Savior has done for them, have refused the benefits of their salvation, refused their inheritance, repudiated the 'hope laid up for [them] in heaven' (Colossians 1:5).

Jesus' atonement has universal intent (Romans 5:18). He died for all and he was raised for all because God so loved the world. He is the 'Lamb of God, who takes away the sin of the world. Scripture shows that God, in Christ, has reconciled all humans to himself (Colossians 1:20); 2 Corinthians 5: 19 but he will never force any person to embrace that reconciliation. Love cannot be coerced.

A relationship of love as the children of God could never be the result of a cause-effect mechanism. God wants sons and daughters who love him out of a joyful response to his love, not zombies who have no mind or choice of their own. As has been revealed in Jesus Christ, God is love in his innermost being, and in God the Persons of the Trinity relate to one another in the truth and freedom of love. That same love is extended to us in Christ that we might share in it, and in nothing less.

To hope that all people will finally come to Christ is not universalism—it is simply Christian and reflects the heart of God (1 Timothy 2:3-6; 2 Peter 3:9). If God calls us to love our enemies, does God himself do less? If God desires that all turn and be saved, can we do anything less?

This does not mean we can profess that every person will finally come to faith and receive their salvation. However this does mean that, given who God is and what he has done for us in Christ, we ought to be more surprised that some may somehow actually come to reject the truth and reality of their salvation than to find many in the end turning to Christ to receive his forgiveness and eternal life as his beloved children.

▪ **Q. If we are reconciled already, why struggle to live the Christian life?**

A. Some people do not like the idea that others who do not work as hard as they do will end up with the same reward as they (see parable of the laborers in the vineyard, Matthew 20:12-15). But this concern overlooks the truth that no one, no matter how hard they work, deserves salvation. That is why it is, for everyone, a free gift.

However, in Scripture we learn that is why God doesn't want us to live that way. Consider the following passages: 'No one can lay any foundation other than the one already laid, which is Jesus Christ. If anyone builds on this foundation using gold, silver, costly stones, wood, hay or straw, their work will be shown for what it is, because the Day will bring it to light. It will be revealed with fire, and the fire will test the quality of each person's work. If what has been built survives, the builder will receive a reward. If it is burned up, the builder will suffer loss but yet will be saved—even though only as one escaping through the flames. (1 Corinthians 3:11-15)

Galatians 6:7-8: 'Do not be deceived: God cannot be mocked. People reap what they sow. Whoever sows to please their flesh, from the flesh will reap destruction; whoever sows to please the Spirit, from the Spirit will reap eternal life.'

We are joined to Christ in order to live in fellowship with Christ. We are united to Christ in order to participate with him in all he does. It makes no more sense to say that since we belong to Christ there is no point in living the Christian life, than to say, since a man and woman are married, there is no point to them living together. No. They are married in order to live together. We are joined to Christ in order to live with him.

- **Q. How do we explain John 6:44?**

A. John 6:44 says, 'No one can come to me unless the Father who sent me draws them.'

The Jewish religious leaders were seeking to deflect Jesus' seemingly outrageous claim: 'I am the bread of life that came down from heaven' (John 6:41). This statement was tantamount to claiming divine status.

Jesus' reply to the Jewish leaders' complaint concerning this claim was that they 'stop grumbling' (verse 43) and realize that 'no one can come to me [the bread of heaven] unless the Father who sent me draws them...' (verse 44). Jesus' point is that the people would not be responding to him, except that God was making it possible for them to do so. If they really knew God they should recognize that people were coming to the Son according to the will and purpose of the Father. What they see happening in Jesus' ministry is not evidence that Jesus is a blasphemer, disobeying the will of God, but rather that God the Father is accomplishing his will through Jesus, his faithful Son.

In this passage, Jesus is not limiting the number of people who are drawn to him; he is showing that he is doing the Father's work. Elsewhere he says: 'When I am lifted up, I will draw all people to myself' (John 12:32). And since Jesus does only what his Father wants, John 12:32 shows that the Father indeed draws all people to Jesus.

- **Q. How does this theology compare to Calvinism and Arminianism?**

A. In comparing and contrasting Christian theologies, we are talking about different approaches or understandings among Christian brothers and sisters who seek to serve the same Lord and thus share the same faith. Thus, our discussion should reflect respect and gentleness, not arrogance or hostility.

Calvinism is a theology that developed from the teachings of the Protestant reformer John Calvin (1509-1564). Calvinism emphasizes the sovereignty of God's will in election and salvation. Most Calvinists define God's 'elect' as a subset of the human race; Christ died for only some people ('limited' or 'particular' atonement). Those elect for whom he did die, however, were truly and effectively saved in the finished work of Christ, long before they became aware of it and accepted it. According to Calvinist doctrine, it is inevitable that those Christ died for will come to faith in him at some point. This is called 'irresistible grace.'

Trinitarian theology's main disagreement with Calvinism is over the scope of reconciliation. Its objection is based on the fundamental fact of who Jesus is and that he is one in will, purpose, mind, authority and act with the Father in the Spirit. The whole God is Savior and Jesus is the new Adam who died for all. The Bible asserts that Christ made atonement 'not only for our sins, but for the sins of the whole world' (1 John 2:2). And while Trinitarian theology rejects the restrictive extent of 'limited atonement' and the determinism of 'irresistible grace,' it agrees with Calvinism that forgiveness, reconciliation, redemption, justification, etc. were all accomplished effectively by what Christ did. And these gospel truths have been secured for us irrespective of our response to them.

Arminianism derives from the teachings of another Protestant reformer, Jacob Arminius (1560-1609). Arminius insisted that Jesus died for all humanity, and that all people can be saved if they take necessary, personal action, which is enabled by the Spirit. This theology, while not ignoring God's sovereignty, gives a more central or key role to human decision and free will. Its premise is that salvation, forgiveness, reconciliation, redemption, justification, etc., are not actually effective unless a person has faith. For only if God foresees a person using their free choice to receive Christ, does he then elect them. Those whom he foresees rejecting his salvation, he condemns. So like the Calvinist, in the end God wills the salvation of some and the condemnation of others.

Trinitarian theology differs from Arminianism over the effectiveness of the reconciliation. Atonement, or at-one-ment between God and humanity, is only a hypothetical possibility for Arminians; it does not become an accomplished actuality unless God foresees someone's decision of faith. In this view God, on the basis of his foreknowledge of an individual's acceptance or rejection, then accepts or rejects that person. Trinitarian theology, however, teaches that the atonement and reconciliation represents the heart and mind of God towards all and is objectively true in Christ, even before it has been subjectively accepted and experienced and remains true even if some deny it. God has one ultimate will or purpose for all, realized from the Father, through the Son and in the Spirit.

While Calvinism and Arminianism emphasize different aspects of salvation theology, Trinitarian theology has attempted, as did Church Fathers Irenaeus, Athanasius, and Gregory, to maintain in harmony the wideness of God's love emphasized by Arminians with the unconditioned faithfulness of God emphasized by Calvinists. But strictly speaking, the Incarnational and Trinitarian theology of GCI aligns neither with traditional Calvinism nor Arminianism. It emphasizes the sovereignty of God's Triune holy love that calls for our response. His sovereign will is expressed in accordance with God's being a fellowship of holy love. Its center is the heart, mind, character and nature of God revealed in the Person and Work of Jesus Christ, the Incarnate Savior and Redeemer. God's sovereignty is most clearly and profoundly shown in Jesus Christ. The place and importance of human response to God's grace is also shown in Jesus Christ who makes a perfect and free response to God in our place and on our behalf as our Great High Priest. Our response then is a gift given by the Holy Spirit by which we share in Christ's perfect response for us in our place and on our behalf.

What on earth is Trinitarian (Christian Hopeful Universalist) Theology?

In my research I found a blog written by John Crowder – a Trinitarian. As I read his thoughts, I felt he accurately reflected the concepts being shared by my friend so I took a moment and made a copy. I shared this with my friend and asked him to read it for me. We later spoke and I asked if the paper was a fair reflection of the positions he held as a "Hopeful Universalist." This term, Hopeful Universalist, is also referred to as, Extreme Grace. My friend defined that term for me as, "I am not a Universalist. But, I am what is called a Hopeful Universalist. In other words, I'm not certain the Universalist position is correct. But I am very hopeful that it is."

He agreed that Mr. Crowder has accurately reflected his view and was especially glad that Mr. Crowder included a section stating their belief was not universalism – for my friend this was an important point. My friend had carefully explained he was not a universalist, however, he was "hopeful" that he was wrong and the universalist was right. Hence the term "hopeful universalist."

For clarity of thought, I have pulled portions of Mr. Crowder's blog and included them in the chapters on Heaven and Hell. The quotes given in those chapters will be attributed to Mr. Crowder. To read the blog in its entirety, please visit, www.gci.org.

- ## Introduction… What on Earth is Trinitarian Theology?

by John Crowder

Because of our scriptural belief that Christ represented all mankind in His vicarious death on the cross, some often confuse this gospel truth with the concept of Universalism. Yes, indeed the cross has universal ramifications. But unfortunately many get mixed up because they are unfamiliar with the grace-based stream of Trinitarian theology. Some of my favorite Trinitarian writers are C.S. Lewis, Fr. Robert Capon, C. Baxter Kruger and perhaps the most prominent theologian of the 20th century, Karl Barth. I am not one who enjoys labels or being pigeonholed by them – but the term 'Trinitarianism' is very loosely knit across many denominational lines. In fact, it is a way of approaching scripture that I find very exhilarating. For those frustrated with the dogmatic, unsatisfying claims of the rigid Calvinism-Arminian-Universalism debate, I think you'll find a refreshing world of truth as you discover there are other options to the theological puzzles on the table.

Why Theology?

Theology, for starters, is 'God knowledge.' For some reason in our charismatic circles, theology gets downplayed – or at least pitted against personal devotion as if it should be frowned upon. Everyone has a theology. Theology is not a problem … it's bad theology that's problematic. Good theology always enhances your joy, fuels the party and guards you against religion, legalism, condemnation and self-destruction! Ultimately, your theology consists of whatever you believe to be true about God. Good theology is never boring … nor is it a waste of time. Barth said, 'Theology is a peculiarly beautiful discipline. Indeed, we can confidently say that it is the most beautiful of all disciplines. To find academic study distasteful is the mark of the Philistine. It is an extreme form of Philistinism to find, or to be able to find, theology distasteful. The theologian who labors without joy is not a theologian at all. Sulky faces, morose thoughts and boring ways of speaking are intolerable in this field.'

Did you know that theology is actually a form of repentance? Repentance, or metanoia, means to 'change your mind.' As we change our mind about the things of God – renewing our thoughts about His goodness and character – His beauty continually manifests in our daily lives.

One common argument is that theology only benefits the mind, whereas God is interested in the heart. I do understand the perils of intellectualism over devotion. But more often than not, we are drawing a false dichotomy between so-called 'head faith' and 'heart faith.' In fact, the same Greek words for heart and mind are consistently interchangeable!

'I believe that many who find that 'nothing happens' when they sit down, or kneel down, to a book of devotion, would find that the heart sings unbidden while they are working their way through a tough bit of theology with a pipe in their teeth and a pencil in their hand,' writes C.S. Lewis (Introduction to On the Incarnation by Athanasius).

Also, keep in mind that theology is a different discipline than Biblical studies. In Biblical studies, you are working through individual passages. Theology, on the other hand, steps back and looks at the whole counsel of scripture – it is concerned with how we approach the whole thing, rightly dividing its entirety from beginning to end so that we can delve comprehensively into the nature and person of God.

Why Trinitarianism?

Okay, let's get one thing straight ... Trinitarianism is not about simply believing in the doctrine of the Trinity! It's a recognition that the Triune God of the Bible is at the heart of all other doctrines and scripture. It means there is a loving Father fully revealed in His Son and made known to us by a very real and present Holy Spirit.

Trinitarianism is not really concerned with the 'how' or 'why' of individual doctrines as much as the 'Who' Get the person and nature of God, and everything else falls into place. Also, to be faithful to the Trinity, we must be Christocentric. We need look no further outside the person of Jesus Christ in order to see who God is – Father, Son and Spirit. The entire Godhead chose to represent Itself through Jesus – to show how passionate God is for us!

Briefly, let me explain three of my own personal reasons for enjoying the Trinitarian approach to theology:

1- Christ as the Ultimate

Text Everyone says, 'I only believe what the Bible says!' What they really mean is that they only believe their own interpretation of the Bible – often very zealously. Yes, the Bible is fully inspired and it's the means by which we see Jesus ... but Jesus Christ – not the Bible - is the ultimate Word of God.

First and foremost, Trinitarian theology is Christ-centered. Every scripture must be read through the lens of the person of Jesus. He said, 'You diligently study the Scriptures because you think that by them you possess eternal life. These are the Scriptures that testify about me, yet you refuse to come to me to have life' (John 5:39-40). Christ is the ultimate text. The full and final revelation of Who God is. Only by looking at Him can we see the true nature of the Godhead. The Father chose to make

Himself known through the Son, and the Spirit constantly points us to Him.

So, in other words, when I read Leviticus, I don't see a big legalistic finger pointing at me, condemning me for my failure at upholding the law. Instead, I see every scripture pointing its finger at Jesus Christ and His finished work. He is the lens through which I read every other text.

Centering everything on Christ changes all our other doctrines. Consider the doctrine of predestination for instance. It's not about God choosing some people and rejecting others. Christ is both the Elector and the Elected. Jesus is God's predestined choice for all of mankind.

Filtering our view of God solely through the revealed Son also means that there is not some other angry God hiding behind Jesus' back, ready to hit me with a lightening (sic) bolt. No dark, impersonal force who stops short of destroying me only because 'He remembers the blood.' Jesus and the Father were not playing 'good cop/bad cop' on the cross. Jesus was not twisting God's arm on the cross, persuading the Father not to destroy you! He was not conditioning or changing God so that He would be gracious to you. The Father was always for you! The heart of the entire Trinity is seen in the work of Christ on the cross. When you look at the love of Jesus dying for you, you are seeing the full expression of the love of the Father as well. Jesus was not changing God's mind about you. God did not need changing – you did! There's no hidden, dark side of God that Jesus was protecting you from. Not some evil "Old Testament" God that needed to be coaxed into loving us.

When Christ is our ultimate lens for understanding scripture, He is also our lens for seeing the unconditional love of the Godhead.

2 – God is Love

Jesus introduces us to the Father. We hear in His words and actions that our Father loves us unconditionally. He did not send Jesus out of anger to punish someone, but rather out of His infinite love and rock-solid commitment to redeem mankind. The Trinitarian approach does not portray a God who loves on some days and hates on other days. God does not love. God is Love. Even the wrath of God is simply an extension of His love. It is a big, fat 'No!' to sinfulness, because of how it destroys and molests His children. God's wrath has nothing to do with hating us. It has to do with hating the sinfulness that was destroying us. Even God's wrath is for you, not against you. The Trinitarian approach sees all scripture through the ultimate grid of God's love.

The Trinitarian approach does not see a moody Father who was personally offended by our sin, requiring the death of His Son to appease His own bloodlust. In fact, the Father never forsook His son on the cross to 'satisfy' His anger. Instead, the Father and Spirit were fully involved on the tree, as 'God was in Christ, reconciling the cosmos to Himself" (2 Corinthians. 5:19). Yes, Jesus entered into our own 'feeling' of separation from God – our own psychological calamity to experience what it's like to feel the consequences of sin. On the cross, He asked the questions you ask ... 'Why have you forsaken me?'... But although he asked your human questions, the Father never did forsake the Son. And the Son never doubted the Father. The Father forsakes no one. The scriptures are clear that the Trinity never turned upon itself on the cross. Jesus and the Father are inseparable, 'I and my Father are one' (John 10:30). And even when He went to the cross, Jesus said, 'You [disciples] will leave me all alone. Yet I am not alone, for my Father is with me'

(John 16:32). To see Jesus on the cross is to see the full loving expression of the Godhead.

Even the most difficult texts about wrath and judgment must ultimately be seen through the lens of 'God is Love' – there is a silver lining of grace behind it all. He is not a schizophrenic deity bouncing between love and hatred. The point of the cross was to redeem mankind from his own self-destruction ... not to pay off an ill-tempered, narcissistic God who was spitting mad at you for sinning against Him.

3 – Dialectical Tension

Many theologies engage in analytical debate against one another with the aim of 'winning' when scriptures seem to present contradictions. Trinitarianism is more mystical – perhaps postmodern in that sense. Rather than debate, it lives in the dialectical tension of mystery. It is okay with embracing paradox.

For instance, there are a plethora of verses on hell and eternal torment. But there are also a plethora of verses on universal salvation for all mankind. Which of these verses do you throw away? Be careful taking scissors to your Bible in any direction! Rather than drawing hard lines of debate, Trinitarian theology holds these things in the tension of paradox, keeping hope for mankind without jumping into dogmatic assumptions. We must look at all sides of scripture to arrive at honest answers. But there are places where your logic (even your best theo-logic) will not provide answers.

In addition, the Trinitarian approach is not 'causal' or problem oriented. It does not start with problems like 'Why aren't some saved?' Instead, it begins with the person and work of Christ, which was sufficient for all men, and works from there as a starting point.

Please enjoy the next extensive article below which is excerpted from the helpful resources of Grace Communion International – it further expands on Trinitarian theology as well as the person and work of Christ. ...

If you enjoyed this article, we suggest you subscribe to The Ecstatic Magazine with a donation of your choosing!

A Brief Introduction to Trinitarian Theology (this was included in the above blog-rs) from Grace Communion International

Historically, Trinitarian theology formed the basis of Christian teaching. This is reflected in the early Christian creeds. Early prominent Trinitarian teachers and theologians included Irenaeus, Athanasius and Gregory of Nazianzus.

Irenaeus (died A.D. 202) was a disciple of Polycarp (who had studied with the apostle John). Irenaeus sought to show that the gospel of salvation taught by the apostles and handed down from them is centered on Jesus. He saw that the Bible presents the Incarnation as a new point of beginning for humanity (see Ephesians 1:9-10, 20-23). Through the Incarnation, the entire human race was 'born again' in Jesus. In Jesus, humanity has a new beginning and a new identity.

The biblical foundation of Irenaeus' thinking included Paul's statements in Romans 5, where Jesus is presented to us as the 'second' (or 'final') Adam of the human race. 'In Jesus,' wrote Irenaeus, 'God recapitulated in Himself the ancient formation of man [Adam], that He might kill sin, deprive death of its power, and vivify man...' (Against Heresies, III.18.7).

Irenaeus understood that Jesus took all humanity into Himself and renewed the human race through his vicarious (representative and substitutionary) life, death, resurrection and ascension.

Irenaeus taught that this renewing, or re-creating, of the human race in Jesus through the Incarnation is not merely a work done 'by' Jesus. Rather, our salvation involves much more than just the forgiveness of our sins. It means our entire re-creation 'in' and 'through' Jesus.

Athanasius (died A.D. 373) defended the gospel against false teachers (including Arius) who denied the Son's eternal divinity. This defense led to the formulation of the doctrine of the Trinity affirmed at the Council of Nicea in A.D. 325. In his treatise On the Incarnation, *section 20, Athanasius wrote the following:*

Thus, taking a body like our own, because all our bodies were liable to the corruption of death, He surrendered His body to death in the place of all, and offered it to the Father. This He did out of sheer love for us, so that in His death all might die…. This He did that He might turn again to incorruption men who had turned back to corruption, and make them alive through death by the appropriation of His body and by the grace of His resurrection…

What then was God to do? What else could He possibly do, being God, but renew His Image in mankind, so that through it men might once more come to know Him? And how could this be done, save by the coming of the very Image Himself, our Savior Jesus Christ? … The Word of God came in His own Person, because it was He alone, the Image of the Father, Who could recreate man made after the Image. Thus it happened that two opposite marvels took place at once: the death of all was consummated in the Lord's body; yet because the Word was in it, death and corruption were in the same act utterly abolished. Death there had to be, and death for all, so that

the due of all might be paid. Wherefore the Word ...
being Himself incapable of death, assumed a mortal body,
that He might offer it as his own in the place of all, and
suffering for the sake of all through His union with it,
'might bring to naught him that had the power over death,
that is, the devil, and might deliver them who all their
lifetime were enslaved by the fear of death' (Hebrews
2:14-15). By his death salvation has come to all men, and
all creation has been redeemed.

Both Athanasius and Irenaeus emphasized the
vicarious nature of the humanity Jesus assumed in his
Incarnation. Only through the birth, life, sacrificial death
and resurrection of the Incarnate Son of God could God
save humanity. This is the essence of the gospel understood
by the early church and revealed in the Scriptures.

Gregory of Nazianzus (died A.D. 389) wrote of
Jesus' assumption of our broken humanity through his
Incarnation:

If anyone has put his trust in Him [Jesus] as a Man
without a human mind, such a person is bereft of mind ...
for that which He has not assumed He has not healed; but
that which is united to His Godhead is also saved. If only
half Adam fell, then that which Christ assumes and saves
may be half also; but if the whole of his nature fell, it
must be united to the whole nature of Him that was
begotten, and so be saved as a whole... (Epistle 101).

"Contemporary Trinitarian theologians

In the 20th century, Trinitarian theology was
advanced in the West largely through the work of Karl
Barth and his students, including three brothers: Thomas
F. Torrance, James B. Torrance and David Torrance, and
their students.

In the 21st century, there are hundreds of
Trinitarian theologians scattered among many

denominations, including Ray Anderson, Elmer Colyer,
Michael Jinkins, C. Baxter Kruger, Alan Torrance, T
Hart and the late Colin Gunton.

Who are you, Lord?

Trinitarian theology faithfully answers the all-
important question: 'Who is Jesus Christ?' Thibiblically
anchored theology adds fullness of understanding to the
gospel—and gives us a Christ-centered vocabulary to share
the gospel with others in our contemporary world.

'Who are you, Lord?' is the principal theological
question. This was Paul's anguished question on the
Damascus Road, where he was struck down by the
resurrected Jesus (Acts 9:5). Paul spent the rest of his life
answering this question and then sharing the answer with
all who would listen. The answer, revealed to us in
Scripture, is the heart of the gospel and the focus of
Trinitarian theology:

Jesus is fully God—the Second Person of the Trinity,
the divine Son of God, in eternal union with the Father
and the Spirit. Scripture tells us that through the Son of
God the entire universe was created, including all humans
(Col. 1:16), and he is the one who sustains the universe,
including all humans (verse 17). So, when we say 'Jesus
Christ' we are also saying 'God' and 'Creator.'

Jesus is fully human—the Son of God (the Word)
became human ('flesh,' John 1:14), while continuing to
remain fully divine. This is called the 'Incarnation.'
Scripture testifies that the Incarnation never ended, but
continues—Jesus is now and forever fully God and fully
human. He was resurrected and ascended bodily. He will
return bodily, the same as he departed. When we say 'Jesus
Christ' we are also saying 'humanity.'

As the One who is uniquely God (Creator and
Sustainer of all) and also fully human, Jesus, in Himself,

is the unique union of God and humanity. In and through the life, death, resurrection and ascension of Jesus all humans are included in the life and love of God. As the apostle Paul emphasized, the man Jesus (1 Timothy 2:5) is the representative and substitute for all people – past, present, and future. He is the vicarious human who has come to live and die and be raised in our place and on our behalf to reconcile us to God – Father, Son and Holy Spirit.

In Romans 5, Paul addresses believers, but what he says applies to all humanity—believers and non-believers alike. Corinthians to Paul, through Jesus, all are…

- *justified through faith, and therefore at peace with God (v. 1)*
- *reconciled to God through the death of Jesus (v. 10)*
- *saved through Jesus' life (v. 10)*

This justification, reconciliation and salvation occurred:

- *when we were 'still powerless' (v. 6)*
- *when we were 'still sinners' (v. 8)*
- *when we were still 'God's enemies' (v. 10)*

This occurred quite apart from our participation, let alone our good works. Jesus did these things for us and to us, and he did it within himself. As Irenaeus said, echoing Ephesians 1:10, it occurred in Jesus, via his Incarnation, through a great "recapitulation."

The benefit of what Jesus did so long ago, extends to the present and on into the future, for Paul says, 'how

*much more…shall we be saved through his life' (v. 10)—
showing that salvation is not a one-time transaction, but an
enduring relationship that God has with all humanity—a
relationship forged within the person of Jesus Christ—the
one who, in himself, has brought God and humanity
together in peace.*

Jesus, the second Adam

*Continuing in Romans 5, Paul compares the first
Adam to Jesus, calling the latter the 'second' or 'final'
Adam. Note Paul's main points:*

- *Just as sin entered the world through one man
  [Adam]… [and] all sinned…' (v. 12)*
- *How much more did God's grace and the gift that
  came by the grace of the one man, Jesus Christ
  [the second Adam], overflow to the many?' (v.
  15)*
- *And, 'just as the result of one trespass [that of
  the first Adam] was condemnation for all men, so
  also the result of one act of righteousness [that of
  Jesus, the second or final Adam] was justification
  that brings life for all men' (v. 18).*

'All' really means 'all'

*Paul is speaking of what Jesus did for all humanity.
The scope of his vicarious human life extends to all who
have ever lived. But not all Christians see 'all' in this way:*

*Calvinism, for example, says salvation is not truly for
all because the atonement is limited to the elect who are
predestined to be saved; Jesus did not die for the non-elect.
However, the Bible declares that Jesus died for all—and
that his death applies to all now. Relevant passages include*

(note: these verses will be addressed in a following chapter, Opinion of the Sages).

- *John 12:32: 'But I [Jesus], when I am lifted up from the earth, will draw all men to myself.'*
- *2 Corinthians 5:14: 'Christ's love compels us, because we are convinced that one died for all, and therefore all died.'*
- *Colossians 1:19-20: 'For God was pleased to have all his fullness dwell in him, and through him to reconcile to himself all things, whether things on earth or things in heaven, by making peace through his blood, shed on the cross.'*
- *1 Timothy 2:3-6: 'This is good, and pleases God our Savior, who wants all men to be saved and to come to a knowledge of the truth. For there is one God and one mediator between God and men, the man Christ Jesus, who gave himself as a ransom for all men.'*
- *1 Timothy 4:9-10: 'This is a trustworthy saying that deserves full acceptance...that we have put our hope in the living God, who is the Savior of all men, and especially of those who believe.'*
- *Hebrews 2:9: 'But we see Jesus, who...suffered death, so that by the grace of God he might taste death for everyone.'*
- *1 John 2:2: '[Jesus is] the atoning sacrifice for our sins, and not only for ours but also for the sins of the whole world.'*

While there is even more evidence, this scriptural evidence is sufficient to conclude that Jesus died for all humanity.

Salvation is re-creation, not mere transaction.

Arminianism, in contrast to Calvinism, agrees that 'all' refers to the entirety of humanity; however, salvation is only potentially theirs, not actually since salvation is not actually given until a person has faith.

But the Bible tells us that salvation does not come about through a mere transaction in which God gives us salvation in exchange for our repentance and faith.

Rather than a transaction, Scripture presents salvation as a free and unearned gift, a gift that involves re-creation. In Jesus, who is fully God and fully human, the perfect representative and substitute for humanity, all humans are a new creation. Although it is experienced only through faith, all humans are justified, reconciled and saved precisely because they are all included in Jesus— included in his Incarnation, life, death, resurrection and ascension.

Jesus did all this for us and to us by doing it with us and in us—as one of us. Jesus is the One for the many, the many in the One. Therefore, we understand from Scripture that…

- *When Jesus died, all humanity died with him.*
- *When Jesus rose, all humanity rose to new life with him.*
- *When Jesus ascended, all humanity ascended and became seated with him at the Father's side.*

Let's evaluate the relevant passages:

- *2 Corinthians 5:14-16: 'For Christ's love compels us, because we are convinced that one died for all, and therefore all died. And he died for all, that those who live should no longer live for themselves but for him who died for them and was raised again.'*

As we saw earlier in Romans 5:18, the result of Jesus' righteousness is 'justification that brings life for all men.' We are told to accept Christ's sacrifice, but this does not cause the sacrifice to be effective; it was already effective.

- *Colossians 1:15-17: 'He [Jesus] is the image of the invisible God, the firstborn over all creation. For by him all things were created: things in heaven and on earth, visible and invisible, whether thrones or powers or rulers or authorities; all things were created by him and for him. He is before all things, and in him all things hold together.'*

Because Jesus is both Creator and Sustainer of the entire cosmos (all humanity included), when he died, all creation (all humans included) 'went down' with him— 'therefore all died' (2 Corinthians 5:14). And when he rose, we all rose; and when he ascended, we all ascended. Jesus includes everyone ('all') in his Incarnation, life, death, burial, resurrection and ascension.

- *Romans 6:10: 'The death he [Jesus] died, he died to sin once for all.' Jesus' death is already effective for everyone; he died to sin once for all.'*
- *Ephesians 2:4-5: 'But because of his great love for us, God, who is rich in mercy, made us alive with Christ even when we were dead in*

> transgressions—it is by grace you have been
> saved.'

- *1 Peter 1:18-20: 'For you know that it was not
  with perishable things such as silver or gold that
  you were redeemed from the empty way of life
  handed down to you...but with the precious blood
  of Christ.... He [Jesus] was chosen [to save
  humanity] before the creation of the world, but
  was revealed in these last times for your sake.'*

The gospel is about a relationship, a relationship with
God healed and made real by God's own action in Christ
on our behalf. It is not about a set of demands, nor is it
about a simple intellectual acceptance of a set of religious
or Bible facts. Jesus Christ not only stood in for us at the
judgment seat of God; he drew us into himself and made
us, with him and in him, by the Spirit, God's own beloved
children.

The one in whom all the cosmos (including all
humanity) lives and moves and has its being (Acts 17:28)
became fully human while remaining fully divine (John
1:14).

Many theologies present a truncated view of the
Incarnation—seeing it as a short-term accommodation by
Jesus to pay the penalty for human sin. But Scripture
presents the Incarnation as ongoing.

The miracle of the Incarnation is not something that
happened 'once upon a time,' now past. It is a change in
how the entire cosmos is 'wired'—it is a new creation (2
Corinthians 5:17). The Incarnation changed everything,
forever—reaching back to all human history, and reaching
forward to encompass all time as it unfolds.

Paul speaks of this in Romans 7:4, where he says
that even while we are alive, we are already dead to the law
by the body of Christ. Jesus' death in human flesh for us,
though a historic event, is a present reality that applies to
all humanity (past, present and future). It is this cosmic
fact that underlies all history. This understanding is
reinforced in Colossians 3:3: 'You died,' Paul says to the
historically alive Colossians, 'and your life is hid with
Christ in God.' Even before we literally die, therefore, we
are already dead in Jesus' death and alive in Jesus'
resurrection.

This is perhaps most clearly stated in Ephesians 2:5-
6, where Paul asserts that since we are dead already in the
mystery of Jesus' substitutionary death, all of us have also
(right now), been 'made alive together with him' and we are
'raised up together with him' and 'seated together with him
in the heavenly realms.' In other words, God in Christ not
only intersects history at one moment of time, but also is
the eternal contemporary of every moment in time, present
there with all humanity included in him.

Perichoresis

The eternal communion of love that Father, Son and
Spirit share as the Trinity involves a mystery of inter-
relationship and interpenetration of the divine Persons, a
mutual indwelling without loss of personal identity. As
Jesus said, '...the Father is in me, and I in the Father'
(John 10:38). Early Greek-speaking Christian
theologians described this relationship with the word
perichoresis, which is derived from root words meaning
around and contain.

Theologian Michael Jinkins comments on how this
perichoretic life involves God's relationship with humanity:
The idea communicated by the word perichoresis is
crucial but difficult to handle. We can best deal with it by

focusing our attention on the incarnation. When the Word became flesh, God poured out his very life into creation while also and simultaneously taking into his own triune being our humanity in the supreme act of self-abnegation for the sake of others. In this free act of self-surrender, God allows us to look into the very heart of his eternal being, into the Father's eternal outpouring into the Son, God's giving away of his own self without reservation. This act of self-giving is itself not merely some 'it' but is God the Holy Spirit, flowing eternally from the Father to the Son and through the Son to humanity. As the Son in joyful surrender returns this love to the Father, the Spirit eternally returns to the Father, the Origin of all being (Invitation to Theology, p. 91).

Everyone is in Christ

In and through Jesus Christ, God reaches out to include humans in his life and love. In and through Jesus, all humanity is now included in the eternal fellowship of the Trinity, although that fellowship can be experienced only through faith.

Jesus said to his followers the night before he died on the cross: 'On that day you will realize that I am in my Father, and you are in me, and I am in you' (John 14:20).

He does not say that one day they will be included—he says they are included and one day they will realize it. Salvation is about being 'in' Jesus, not merely something being done 'by' Jesus, which we later accept and thus make it 'real' or 'actual' for us. Salvation is about a relationship, and that is why Paul so frequently in his letters (over 130 times) speaks of something being 'in Christ' or similar phrases.

Salvation is ours only in union with Jesus, by which we share in Jesus' perfect human life and his relationship to the Father and the Spirit. United to Jesus, we are already included in God's triune life and love. But we cannot experience the joy of that life apart from faith.

As we have seen in Scripture, through union with Jesus, all humanity is…

- *Reconciled to the Father.*
- *Liked, loved and wanted by the Father.*
- *Accepted 'in the Beloved' (Ephesians 1:6, KJV).*
- *Forgiven (no… sin and no condemnation).*

The gospel declares not the possibility or the potential of these things being true for us, but a reality that we are urged to accept.

The faith of Christ

In the King James Version, Galatians 2:20 reads: 'I am crucified with Christ: nevertheless I live; yet not I, but Christ liveth in me: and the life which I now live in the flesh I live by the faith of the Son of God, who loved me, and gave himself for me.'

This and other translations speak appropriately of our sharing in the faith of Christ (rather than 'faith in Christ'). It is Christ's faith that saves us. David Torrance writes (emphasis added):

We are saved by Christ's faith and obedience to the Father, not ours. My brother Tom [Torrance] often quoted Galatians 2:20…. Such is the wording of the KJV, which I believe is a correct translation…. Other translators, like those of the New International Version, apparently because they found it so difficult to believe we can live by Christ's faith rather than our faith, have altered the text to make it read, 'I live by faith in the Son of God' – something altogether different! That translation takes away from the vicarious nature of Christ's life of faith. It is by his faith [not ours] that we are saved and live! Our faith is a thankful response to his faith. When we look back along our lives and ponder how disobedient we at times have been and continue to be, it is marvelously comforting to know that Christ gives us his life of obedience to the Father and that it is Christ's obedience which counts. We are saved by his obedience, not ours. (An Introduction to Torrance Theology, *pp. 7-8)*

Thomas Torrance writes:

'Jesus steps into the actual situation where we are summoned to have faith in God, to believe and trust in him, and he acts in our place and in our stead from within the depths of our unfaithfulness and provides us freely with a faithfulness in which we may share.... That is to say, if we think of belief, trust or faith as forms of human activity before God, then we must think of Jesus Christ as believing, trusting, or having faith in God the Father on our behalf and in our place. ... Through his incarnational and atoning union with us our faith is implicated in his faith, and through that implication, far from being depersonalized or dehumanized, it is made to issue freely and spontaneously out of our own human life before God. Regarded merely in itself, however as Calvin used to say, faith is an empty vessel, for in faith it is upon the faithfulness of Christ that we rest and even the way in which we rest on his is sustained and undergirded by his unfailing faithfulness' (The Mediation of Christ, pp. 82-83).

But what about human freedom?

If it is the life, faith and obedience of Jesus Christ that saves us and includes us in that salvation, what is our role? What happens in this viewpoint to the idea of human freedom? Consider the following points:

- *All humanity, by God's sovereign decision and action, is included in Christ; this inclusion was predestined and has been accomplished in Jesus, apart from any action, belief, works, etc. of our own.*

- *Each person is now urged, through the prompting of the Spirit, to believe God's word and personally accept his love.*

- *God forces this personal decision/ acceptance upon no one. Love must be freely given and freely received; it cannot be coerced, or it is not love.*

- *Thus human decision, the exercise of human freedom, is of great importance, but only in this context of accepting God's gift that has already been freely given.*

Not universalism

When we talk about human decision, we are talking about personal response. And we must take care not to confuse what is objectively true in Jesus for all humanity with an individual's personal and subjective reception of or encounter with this objective truth.

- *We do not 'decide for Christ' in the sense that our personal decision creates or causes our salvation.*

- *Rather, through personal decision, we accept what is ours already in Christ, placing our trust in the one who has already trusted for us in our place and as our representative.*

- *The Holy Spirit leads us to trust not in our faith, but in Jesus.*

- *This objective union, which we have with Christ through his incarnational assumption of our* humanity into himself, is personally and subjectively lived out in faith through the indwelling Holy Spirit.

- When we personally believe the gospel, which is to accept what is already ours by grace, we begin to enjoy God's love for us and live out the new creation that God, prior to our ever believing, made us to be in Christ.

There is the general, or objective, truth about all humanity in Jesus, and also the personal, or subjective, experience of this truth.

Objectively all people, past, present and future, are justified already; all are sanctified; all are reconciled in Jesus in and through what he has done as their representative and substitute. In Jesus, objectively, the old self has already passed away; in him, objectively, we are already the new humanity, represented as such by him before and with God.

However, although all people are already objectively redeemed by Jesus Christ, not all have yet personally and subjectively awakened to and accepted what God has done for them. They do not yet know who they truly are in union with Jesus.

What is objectively true for everyone must be subjectively and personally received and experienced through repentance and faith. Repentance and faith do not create or cause a person's salvation, but salvation cannot be experienced and enjoyed without them. Repentance and faith are themselves gifts of God.

In the Scriptures, we find some verses that speak to the general/objective, while others speak to the personal/subjective. Both are real and true—but the personal is true only because the general is a pre-existing reality.

These two categories are found throughout Scripture—both sometimes occurring in one passage, as happens in 2 Corinthians 5:18-21. Paul starts in verses 18-19 with the objective/universal: 'All this is from God, who reconciled [past tense] us to himself through Christ and gave us the ministry of reconciliation: that God was reconciling the world to himself in Christ, not counting men's sins against them. And he has committed to us the message of reconciliation.'

Good news for all people

Here is a general truth that applies objectively to all—all are already reconciled to God through what Jesus has done in union with all humanity.

Any theology that is faithful to Scripture and to Jesus himself must account for this truth. Unfortunately, many theologies tend to ignore this aspect and focus primarily or only on the personal/subjective. That does the gospel a disservice, because it is the general/objective aspect of who Jesus is and what he has done that is the foundation upon which the personal/subjective rests.

Back to 2 Corinthians 5, having established the general in verses 18-21, Paul goes on in verses 20-21 to address the subjective/personal: 'We are therefore Christ's ambassadors, as though God were making his appeal through us. We implore you on Christ's behalf: Be reconciled to God. God made him who had no sin to be sin for us.'

How can all be 'reconciled' already and yet the invitation go out to 'be reconciled'—suggesting a reconciliation yet to occur? The answer is that both are true—these are two aspects of one truth. All are already reconciled in Christ—this is the universal and objective *truth—but not all yet embrace and therefore experience their reconciliation with God.*

To be reconciled, and yet not know and experience it, is to continue to live as though one is not reconciled. Having one's eyes opened by the Spirit to this reconciliation, choosing to embrace it, and then experiencing it does not cause the reconciliation to occur, but it does make it personally realized. Thus, the evangelistic invitation from Christ's ambassadors (verse 20) is to 'be reconciled.' But this appeal is not to do something that would bring about reconciliation; rather it is an appeal to receive the reconciliation that exists already with God in Christ.

For more resources from Grace Communion International, visit them online at www.gci.org.

John Crowder, 3/1/2012

Contemporary Issues with Trinitarian Doctrine

You may have heard of the controversy surrounding Pastor Rob Bell, mega-church pastor, author, and conference speaker. Bell wrote a book in which he espouses and articulates the doctrine of the Trinitarian position entitled, "Love Wins."

An immediate turmoil surrounded him. Fellow Christian leaders were quick to respond, many standing on the historical side of Christianity, while others were thankful that he had so clearly and publicly expressed their beliefs. The controversy was so pronounced that it became a source of commentary for public news and television personalities like Oprah Winfrey.

The "truth" espoused by the Trinitarian is very good news for the non-Christian world. It is an all-inclusive position absent of the wrath of God towards mankind. It removes the stigma and division created by some overly zealous and predominately legalistic religious people and groups. As a result, it is truly good news for all people.

I will tell you that my friend did not read the book. He had heard the position it stated, he knew the cost to Mr. Bell and my friend did not want to cloud his mind during his search for truth. After much encouragement from me, he finally read a "cliff-note" version of the book. He later told me he found many points of agreement and felt the book clearly expressed many of the thoughts, beliefs, and positions he had espoused during his own journey.

I do not view myself as a scholar, instead I am one who reads what the scholars have said. I endeavor to research the minds of the theologians, and the words of the scholars. I apply the inductive method of systematic theology study as described by Dr. Hodge; the result has become my doctrinal belief system for a systematic theology.

As part of my research in Trinitarianism, I read a blog by Kevin DeYoung, an evaluation of Bell's book, "Love Wins". I have found his thoughts to be in agreement with my own regarding Trinitarianism. Below, I am including his blog. It is too long to include it in the entirety of this writing. So, I have included the site address where you can go and read it in its entirety.

Following is a review by Kevin DeYoung on Rob Bell's book, "Love Wins." A book written from the Trinitarian perspective. As stated, I will only quote portions. However, you can go online and search for, God Is Still Holy… By Kevin DeYoung, thegospelcoalition.org/blogs/kevindeyoung Copyright (c) Kevin DeYoung 2011) to read the article in its entirety.

Mr. DeYoung writes:

> *Love Wins, by megachurch pastor Rob Bell, is, as the subtitle suggests, 'a book about heaven, hell, and the fate of every person who ever lived.' Here's the gist: Hell is what we create for ourselves when we reject God's love. Hell is both a present reality for those who resist God and a future reality for those who die unready for God's love. Hell is what we make of heaven when we cannot accept the good news of God's forgiveness and mercy. But hell is not forever. God will have his way. How can his good purposes fail? Every sinner will turn to God and realize he has already been reconciled to God, in this life or in the next...*
>
> *Unfortunately, beyond this, there are dozens of problems with Love Wins. The theology is heterodox. The*

history is inaccurate. The impact on souls is devastating. And the use of Scripture is indefensible. Worst of all, Love Wins demeans the cross and misrepresents God's character.

… Judgmentalism is not the same as making judgments. The same Jesus who said 'do not judge' in Matthew 7:1, calls his opponents dogs and pigs in Matthew 7:6. Paul pronounces an anathema on those who preach a false gospel (Galatians 1:8). Disagreement among professing Christians is not a plague on the church. In fact, it is sometimes necessary…

… this is not an evangelistic work, not in the traditional sense anyway. The primary intended audience appears to be not so much secularists with objections to Christianity (á la Keller's Reason for God), but disaffected evangelicals who can't accept the doctrine they grew up with. Bell writes for the 'growing number' who have become aware that the Christian story has been 'hijacked' (vii). Love Wins is for those who have heard a version of the gospel that now makes their stomachs churn and their pulses rise, and makes them cry out, 'I would never be a part of that' (viii)…

… Love Wins has ignited such a firestorm of controversy because it's the current fissure point for a larger fault-line. As younger generations come up against an increasingly hostile cultural environment, they are breaking in one of two directions—back to robust orthodoxy (often Reformed) or back to liberalism.

… Love Wins is such a departure from historic Christianity, that there's no easy way to tackle it. You can't point to two or three main problems or three or four exegetical missteps. This is a markedly different telling of the gospel from start to finish.

… *Bell's view of traditional evangelical theology, history, exegesis, eschatology, Christology, gospel, and God... A staggering number of people have been taught that a select few Christians will spend forever in a peaceful, joyous place called heaven while the rest of humanity spends forever in torment and punishment in hell with no chance for anything better. It's been clearly communicated to many that this belief is a central truth of the Christian faith and to reject it is, in essence, to reject Jesus. This is misguided, toxic, and ultimately subverts the contagious spread of Jesus' message of love, peace, forgiveness and joy that our world desperately needs to hear.*

Later, Bell allows that traditionalists can believe their story of heaven and hell, but 'it isn't a very good story' (110). Traditional Christians have inferior news to share because in their story so many people end up in hell. 'That's why the Christians who talk the most about going to heaven while everybody else goes to hell don't throw very good parties' (179). Not only are they bad at parties, traditionalists are bad at art: 'An entrance understanding of the gospel... It's a cheap view of the world because it's a cheap view of God. It's a shriveled imagination' (180).

… *Again, we sense Bell is trying to reconcile an earlier faith with his present trajectory. The result is an awkward attempt to claim his past while still wanting to evolve out of it. This presumes, of course, that the Christian faith is not a deposit to guard or a tradition that must not change (2 Timothy 1:14; 2 Thessalonians. 2:15). Much of Bell's polemic fails if there is a core of apostolic teaching that we are called, not just to embrace as part of our journey, but to protect from deviation and defend against false teaching (Acts 20:29–31).*

Historical Problems Bell maintains he is not saying anything new. And that's right. The problem is he makes it sound like his everyone-ends-up-restored-and-reconciled-to-God theology is smack dab in the center of the Christian tradition.

And so, beginning with the early church, there is a long tradition of Christians who believe that God will ultimately restore everything and everybody, because Jesus says in Matthew 19 that there will be a 'renewal of all things,' Peter says in Acts 3 that Jesus will 'restore everything,' and Paul says in Colossians 1 that through Christ 'God was pleased to. . .. reconcile to himself all things, whether things on earth or things in heaven.' (107, ellipsis in original)

It's important to Bell that he falls within the 'deep, wide, diverse stream' of 'historic, orthodox Christian faith' (ix-x). Therefore, he argues that 'at the center of the Christian tradition since the first church has been the insistence that history is not tragic, hell is not forever, and love, in the end, wins' (109).

This bold claim flies in the face of Richard Bauckham's historical survey: Until the nineteenth century almost all Christian theologians taught the reality of eternal torment in hell. Here and there, outside the theological mainstream, were some who believed that the wicked would be finally annihilated. . .. Even fewer were the advocates of universal salvation, though these few included some major theologians of the early church. Eternal punishment was firmly asserted in official creeds and confessions of the churches. It must have seemed as indispensable a part of the universal Christian belief as the doctrines of the Trinity and the incarnation. ('Universalism: A Historical Survey,' Themelios 4.2 [September 1978]: 47–54)

Universalism (though in a different form than Bell's and for different reasons) has been present in the church since Origen, but it was never in the center of the tradition. Origen's theology was partly anticipated by his fellow Platonist Clement of Alexandria and later shows up in the Cappadocian Gregory of Nyssa. But according to William Moore and Henry Austin Wilson in the Nicene and Post-Nicene Fathers series, Gregory's theology of hell is hard to pin down. He makes much of God being 'all in all' and evil being eradicated, but he also warns of the final judgment and the flames ready to engulf the wicked (NPNF ser. 2, 5:16). Whatever Origen's influence on the Cappadocian fathers (and it was considerable), Origen's views were later refuted by Augustine and, as Bauckham notes, condemned in 543 in a council at Constantinople.

Bell also mentions Jerome, Basil, and Augustine because they claimed many people in their day believed in the ultimate reconciliation of all people to God (107). But listing all the heavyweights who took time to refute the position you are now espousing is not a point in your favor...

... Every point of Christian doctrine has been contested, but some have been deemed heterodox. Universalism, traditionally, was considered one of those points. True, many recent liberal theologians have argued for versions of universalism—and this is where Bell stands, not in the center of the historic Christian tradition.

... Bell cites Psalm 65, Ezekiel 36, Isaiah, Zephaniah, Philippians 2, and Psalm 22 to show that all peoples will eventually be reconciled to God. He does not mention that some of these are promises to God's people, some are general promises about the nations coming to God, and others are about the universal acknowledgement (not to be equated with saving faith) on the last day that Jesus Christ is Lord. Not one of his texts supports his conclusion.

... Bell lists a number of passages that point to final restoration—Jeremiah 5, Lamentations 3, Hosea 14, Zephaniah 3, Isaiah 57, Hosea 6, Joel 3, Amos 9, Nahum 2, Zephaniah 2, Zephaniah 3, Zechariah 9, Zechariah 10, and Micah 7 (86–87). Anyone familiar with the prophets knows that they often finish with a promise of future blessing. But anyone familiar with the prophets should also know that these promises are for God's covenant people, predicated on faith and repentance, and fulfilled ultimately in Christ.

... Bell seems to recognize the covenantal nature of the promised restoration ... To prove this point, he cites a passage from Isaiah 19 where it is predicted that an altar to the Lord will be in the midst of the land of Egypt. Bell concludes that no failure is final and that consequences can always be corrected (88–89). But Isaiah 19 is not remotely about postmortem opportunities to repent. The text is about God's plan to humble Egypt to the point where they cry out to Israel's God for deliverance... God makes no promise that every soul in Egypt will be saved. Rather he promises, like the prophets do time and time again, that if they call on the Lord he will have mercy on them. There is no thought that they will do this calling in the afterlife.

... Bell makes no attempt to understand John 14:6 in context. After acknowledging that Jesus is the way, the truth, and the life and the only way to the Father, Bell quickly adds, 'What he doesn't say is how, or when, or in what manner the mechanism functions that gets people to God through Jesus. He doesn't even state that those coming to the Father through Jesus will even know that they are coming exclusively through him. He simply claims that whatever God is doing in the world to know and redeem and love and restore the world is happening through him'

(154). Even a cursory glance at John 14 shows that the *through* in verse 16 refers to faith. The chapter begins by saying, 'Believe in God; believe also in me.' ... Coming to the Father through Christ means through faith in Christ. This is in keeping with the overall purpose of John's gospel (John 20:31).

... Bell thinks the rich man's question 'What must I do to inherit eternal life?' has nothing to do with the afterlife. He isn't asking about how to go to heaven when he dies (30). He's simply wondering how to get in on the good things God is doing in the age to come (31, 40). Again, Bell ignores all contextual clues to the contrary. Given the resurrection discussion alive in Jesus' day (see Mark 12:18–27), the rich man is likely asking, 'How can I be sure I'll be saved in the final resurrection?' He is thinking of life after death. That's why he says 'inherit' and why the previous section in Mark discusses Bell's dreaded 'entrance' theology (Mark 10:13–16).

... Bell reads too much into Paul's discipline passages. Paul handed over Hymenaeus and Alexander to teach them not to blaspheme. He disciplined the man in Corinth so that his spirit may be saved on the day of the Lord. Therefore, Bell reasons, failure is never final (89–90). But stating the purpose and hope of discipline (as Paul does) is one thing, assuming the repentance happened is another, and thinking any of this opens the door to postmortem second chances is a thing the text never hints at.

... Bell cites Jesus' words in John 3:17 that he 'did not come to judge the world but to save it' (160). This Jesus, Bell says, is a 'vast, expansive, generous mystery' leading us to conclude hopefully that 'Heaven is, after all, full of surprises.' Bell's lean into universalism here would be significantly muted had he gone on to Jesus' words in *verse 18: 'Whoever believes in him [i.e., the Son] is not condemned, but whoever does not believe is condemned already, because he has not believed in the name of the only Son of God.' Likewise, according to John 3:36, 'Whoever believes in the Son has eternal life; whoever does not obey the Son shall not see life, but the wrath of God remains on him.'*

... Bell's overview of Revelation skims along the surface of the book in a way that misses all the hard parts he doesn't want to see... he says, 'the letter does not end with blood and violence' (112). It ends with the world permeated with God's love (114).

... he explains the judgments by reminding us that people often reject the love and joy in front of them and 'choose to live in their own hells all the time' (114). But even a cursory read through Revelation shows that violent judgments issue from God's throne. They are poured out from bowls and thrown down on the earth. Christ comes on a war horse with a sharp sword in his mouth. There's no sense that the wicked are suffering only from their poor decisions in life. They wail for fear because the one whom they pierced is coming with the clouds for recompense (Revelations. 1:7).

... Bell suggests that maybe the gates in heaven are 'never shut' because new citizens will continue to enter the city as everyone is eventually reconciled to God (115). This interpretation is clearly at odds with the rest of Revelation 21-22 which emphasizes several times that there are some accursed ones left outside the city (21:8, 27; 22:3, 14–15, 18–19). The theme of judgment carries through right to the end of the book. What's more, those facing this judgment will be thrown into the lake of fire where torment never ends, which is the second death (20:10; 21:8). There is never a hint of postmortem second chances

and every indication of an irreversible judgment decreed of every soul at the end of the age.

... according to Bell, the announcement 'I am making all things new' suggests new possibilities. This, in turn, means we should leave the door open that the final eternal state of every person has not been fixed (116).

... what Bell does with Sodom and Gomorrah should make even his most ardent supporters wince... In one place, Bell argues from Ezekiel 16 that because the fortunes of Sodom will be restored (Ezekiel. 16:53), this suggests that the forever destiny of others might end in restoration (84). But it should be obvious that the restoration of Sodom in Ezekiel is about the city, not about the individual inhabitants of the town who were already judged in Genesis 19... If that weren't bad enough, the other discussion on Sodom is even worse. Because Jesus says it will be more bearable for Sodom on the day of judgment than for Capernaum (Matthew. 11:23–24), Bell concludes that there is hope for all the other Sodoms and Gomorrahs (85). Bell takes a passage about judgment—judgment that will be so bad for Capernaum it's even worse than God's judgment on Sodom—and turns it into tacit support for ultimate universalism.

... not surprisingly, Bell frequently harkens back to the Pauline promise in Ephesians 1 and Colossians 1 that God is reconciling or uniting all things together in Christ (149). These are favorite passages of universalists, but they cannot carry the freight universalists want them to. Take Ephesians 1, for example. Paul says that God's plan in the fullness of time is to unite all things in Christ, things in heaven and things on earth (Ephesians 1:10). The Greek word for 'unite' is a long one: anakephalaiōsasthai. It means to sum up, to bring together

to a main point, to gather together. It is like an author finishing the last chapter of his book or a conductor bringing the symphony from cacophony to harmony. It's a glorious promise, already begun in some ways by the word of Christ. But we know from the rest of Ephesians that Paul does not expect all peoples to be reconciled to God. He speaks of sons of disobedience and children of wrath in chapter two. In chapter five, he makes clear that the sexually immoral and covetous have no inheritance in the kingdom of Christ. In Ephesians 5:6 he warns that the wrath of God comes upon the sons of disobedience. The uniting of all things does not entail the salvation of all people. It means that everything in the universe, heaven and earth, the spiritual world and the physical world, will finally submit to the lordship of Christ, some in joyful worship of their beloved Savior and others in just punishment for their wretched treason. In the end, God wins.

... his use of Scripture... it is naïve, literalistic Biblicism. He flattens everything, either to make traditional theology sound ridiculously inconsistent or to make a massive point from one out of context verse. He makes no attempt to understand metaphors, genre, or imagery (either in Scripture or in his grandmother's painting). He does not try to harmonize anything that might rot his fresh take on the Bible.

... Bell sounds like an overwrought preterist at times, having no place for end-times judgment or an unending existence after death. But on the other hand, he seems to leave all these arguments behind later when he talks about an eternal postmortem existence. He does believe in heaven after you die, and he believes in hell.

But in a strange bit of logic arising out of the parable of the prodigal son, Bell maintains that heaven and hell exist side by side. It's not always clear what Bell thinks, but it seems he believes everyone goes to the same realm when they die; but for some people it is heaven, and for others it is hell (170). If you don't accept God's story about the world and resist his love, heaven will be hell for you, a hell you create for yourself. We are supposed to see this in Luke 15 where both brothers are invited to the same feast but one can't enjoy it. Heaven and hell at the same party (176).

Bell seems unaware that theologians of various traditions have talked about the two sides of God's will (or two lenses through which God views the world). To be sure, there is mystery here, but it's common to distinguish between God's will of decree, whereby everything that he wills comes to pass (Ephesians 1:11), and his will of desire which can be rejected (Matthew. 7:21). And yet one of Bell's main planks in support of universal reconciliation is that if God wants all people to be saved, then all people must eventually be saved.

All this is built on the statement that God wants everyone to be saved. There's no exegetical work on the meaning of 'all people' and no discussion on the dual-nature of God's will. In Bell's mind, if all people do not end up reconciled to God its tantamount to God saying, 'Well, I tried, I gave it my best shot, and sometimes you just have to be okay with failure' (103). Bell has taken one statement from 1 Timothy 2:4 (God desires all people to be saved), avoids any contextual work on the passage (e.g., all probably means 'all kinds of people'), and refuses to bring any other relevant passages to bear on this one (e.g., Romans 9:22, 'What if God desiring to show his wrath and make known his power, has endured with much patience vessels of wrath prepared for destruction?') The result is a simplistic formula: 'God wants all people to be *saved. God gets what he wants. Therefore, all people will eventually be saved.' ... If it is 'the will of God' that Christians 'abstain from sexual immorality' (1 Thessalonians. 4:3), does that mean God's greatness is diminished by our impurity?*

... Now it's true, Bell believes in hell. But he does not believe that God pours out his wrath on anyone forever (I'm not sure he thinks God actively pours out wrath on anyone at all). Hell is the sad suffering of this life (71). Hell is God giving us what we want (72). Postmortem hell is what we create for ourselves when we refuse to believe God's story, when we resist his love (170-71, 172, 177). There is hell now and hell later. There are all kinds of hell because there are all kinds of ways to reject the good and the true and the beautiful and the human now, in this life, and so we can only assume we can do the same in the next' (79).

... For Bell, this life is about getting ourselves fitted for the good life to come. Some of us die ready to experience God's love. Others need more time to sort things out... 'No one can resist God's pursuit forever because God's love will eventually melt even the hardest hearts' (108).

... In Bell's theology, ultimately, everyone will be saved. If he's right, most of church history has been wrong. If he's wrong, a staggering number of people are hearing 'peace, peace' where there is no peace.

... Bell assumes all sorts of things that can't be shown from Scripture. For example, Bell figures God won't say 'sorry, too late' to those in hell who are humble and broken for their sins. But where does the Bible teach the damned are truly humble or penitent? For that matter, where does the Bible talk about growing and maturing in the afterlife or getting a second chance after death? Why does the Bible make such a big deal about repenting 'today'

(Hebrews? 3:13), about being found blameless on the day of Christ (2 Peter 3:14), about not neglecting such a great salvation (Hebrews. 2:3) if we have all sorts of time to figure things out in the next life? Why warn about not inheriting the kingdom (1 Corinthians. 6:9–10), about what a fearful thing it is to fall into the hands of the living God (Hebrews. 10:31), or about the vengeance of our coming King (2 Thessalonians. 1:5–12) if hell is just what we make of heaven? Bell does nothing to answer these questions, or even ask them in the first place.

… according to Bell, salvation is realizing you're already saved. We are all forgiven. We are all loved, equally and fully by God who has made peace with everyone. That work is done. Now we are invited to believe that story and live in it (172–73).

Bell is not saying what you think he might be saying. He's not suggesting faith is the instrumental cause used by the Spirit to join us to Christ so we can share in all his benefits. That would be evangelical theology. Bell is saying God has already forgiven us whether we ask for it or not, whether we repent and believe or not, whether we are born again or not. 'Forgiveness is unilateral. God isn't waiting for us to get it together, to clean up, shape up, get up—God has already done it' (189). This means the Father's love just is. It cannot be earned and it cannot be taken away. God's love is simply yours (188). Heaven and hell (however Bell conceives them) are both full of forgiven people.

So what does Bell believe about the atonement?… Jesus' sacrifice on the cross was a generic doing-away of all sacrifices. It means 'no more wondering if the gods were pleased with you and or ready to strike you down' (125). Notice, Bell does not say that Jesus' death appeased the anger of God/gods, only that his sacrifice shows us we don't have to wonder any more if the gods are angry. Sacrifice, whether in the Old Testament or on the cross, is not about loving divine self-substitution, but the divine manifestation of love already present in the world, a love whose only obstacle is our ignorance of it and unwillingness to receive it.

Bell categorically rejects any notion of penal substitution. It simply does not work in his system or with his view of God. 'Let's be very clear, then,' Bell states, 'we do not need to be rescued from God. God is the one who rescues us from death, sin, and destruction. God is the rescuer' (182). I see no place in Bell's theology for Christ the curse-bearer (Galatians 3:13), or Christ wounded for our transgressions and crushed by God for our iniquities (Isaiah 53:5, 10), no place for the Son of Man who gave his life as a ransom for many (Mark 10:45), no place for the Savior who was made sin for us (2 Corinthians. 5:21), no place for the sorrowful suffering Servant who drank the bitter cup of God's wrath for our sake (Mark 14:36).

In Bell's theology, God is love, a love that never burns hot with anger and a love that cannot distinguish or discriminate. 'Jesus' story,' Bell says, 'is first and foremost about the love of God for every single one of us. It is a stunning, beautiful, expansive love and it is for everybody, everywhere' (vii). Therefore, he reasons, 'we cannot claim him to be ours any more than he's anybody else's' (152). This is tragic. It's as if Bell wants every earthly father to love every child in the world in the exact same way. If you rob a father of his unique, specific, not-for-everyone love, you rob the children of their greatest treasure.

... If Bell is right, then historic orthodoxy is toxic and terrible. But if the traditional view of heaven and hell are right, Bell is blaspheming. I do not use the word lightly...

... *Millions have been taught that if they don't believe, if they don't accept in the right way according to the person telling them the gospel, and they were hit by a car and died later that same day, God would have no choice but to punish them forever in conscious torment in hell. God would, in essence, become a fundamentally different being to them in that moment of death, a different being to them forever. A loving heavenly father who will go to extraordinary lengths to have a relationship with them would, in the blink of an eye, become a cruel, mean, vicious tormenter who would insure that they would have no escape from an endless future of agony.*

If there was an earthly father who was like that, we would call the authorities. If there was an actual human dad who was that volatile, we would contact child protection services immediately… If God can switch gears like that, switch entire modes of being that quickly, that raises a thousand questions about whether a being like this could ever be trusted. Let alone be good. Loving one moment, vicious the next. Kind and compassionate, only to become cruel and relentless in the blink of an eye.

That kind of God is simply devastating. Psychologically crushing. We can't bear it. No one can. . .. That God is terrifying and traumatizing and unbearable. (173–75)

... *In Bell's telling of the story, there is no sense of the vertical dimension of our evil. Yes, Bell admits several times that we can resist or reject God's love. But there's never any discussion of the way we've offended God, no suggestion that ultimately all our failings are a failure to worship God as we should. God is not simply disappointed with our choices or angry for the way we judge others. He is angry at the way we judge him. He cannot stand to look upon our uncleanness. His nostrils flare at iniquity. He hates our ingratitude, our impurity, our Godcomplexes (sic), our self-centeredness, our disobedience, our despising of his holy law. Only when we see God's eye-covering holiness will we grasp the magnitude of our traitorous rebellion, and only then will we marvel at the incomprehensible love that purchased our deliverance on the cross.*

Bell begins the book by noting how fed up he is with the traditional story about Jesus. He insists on telling a different story... (but)... Look at God's people in the garden, then kicked out of the garden; God's people in the promised land, then booted out of the promised land; God's people in the New Jerusalem, then the wicked and unbelieving locked outside the New Jerusalem. Trace this story from tabernacle to temple through the incarnation and Pentecost and the coming down of the new heaven and new earth and you will see that the Bible's story is about how a holy God can possibly dwell among an unholy people. The good news of this story is not that God loves everybody everywhere and you just need to find Christ in the rocks all around you. The good news is that God over and over makes a way for his unholy people to dwell in his holy presence, and that all these ways were pointing to the one Way, our Lord and Savior Jesus Christ.

... Hell is not what we make for ourselves or gladly choose. It's what a holy God justly gives to those who exchange the truth of God for a lie. The bowls of wrath in Revelations are poured out by God; they are not swum in by sinners. The ten plagues were sent by God; they were not the product of some Egyptian spell gone wrong. God's wrath burns against the impenitent and unbelieving; they do not walk into the fire by themselves.

Bell's god is wholly passive toward sin... There's no way to make sense of Nadab and Abihu or Perrez-

Uzzah or Gehazi or Achan's or Korah's rebellion or the flood or the exodus or the Babylonian captivity or the preaching of John the Baptist or the visions of Revelation or the admonitions of Paul or the warnings of Hebrews or Calvary's cross apart from a God who hates sin, judges sin, and pour out his wrath—sometimes now, always later—on the accursed things and peoples of this world. God is God and there is no hope for non-gods who want to be gods, except through the God-man who became a curse for us.

... The second chances are good not just for this life, but for the next. And what if they aren't? What if Jesus says on the day of judgment, 'Depart from me, I never knew you' (Matthew. 7:23)? What if at the end of the age the wicked and unbelieving cry out, 'Fall on us and hide us from the face of him who sits on the throne, and from the wrath of the Lamb' (Revelation 6:16)? What if outside the walls of the New Jerusalem 'are the dogs and sorcerers and the sexually immoral and murderers and idolaters, and everyone who loves and practices falsehood' (Revelations. 22:15)? What if there really is only one name 'under heaven given among men by which we must be saved' (Acts 4:12)? And what if the wrath of God really remains on those who do not believe in the Son (John 3:18, 36)?

If Love Wins" is wrong—if the theology departs from the apostolic good deposit, if the biblical reasoning falls short in a hundred places, if the god of "Love Wins" and the gospel of "Love Wins" are profoundly mistaken—if all this is true, then what damage has been done to the souls of men and women?

Bad theology hurts real people. So of all the questions raised in the book, the most important question every reader must answer is this: is it true?... Is "Love

Wins" true to the word of God? That's the issue. Open a Bible, pray to God, listen to the faithful Christians of the past 2000 years, and answer the question for yourself.

Questions and Thoughts Needing a Response From the Trinitarian

Perhaps your mind has developed questions as you have been reading. I certainly hope so. It would be unusual to have read conflicting viewpoints without questions being raised by an engaged reader. The following pages will examine questions I too have had, some still requiring an answer.

There may be some who are at a tipping point in their faith and will lean toward Trinitarianism. If so, please take time to research the preponderance of theologians for an answer. Open your Bible, pray, search the scholars of the past 2000 years, and allow God to reveal His truth.

Others may stand on this important eternal truth just because that is what they have been told to do. At some point faith, needs to move from "doctrine that I accept", to "doctrine that I believe."

I begin this Q/A section with an excerpt from the writings of Thomas Talbott, an advocate for the Trinitarian Universalist position. In this passage, he deals with issues that the Trinitarian believer must grapple with in their belief system. Talbott shares what, to him, are answers to these problematic subjects. I include his thoughts for a fair and balanced approach to my questions in order to allow him to share his answers in order to help the reader discern the truth.

Thomas Talbott, himself an advocate of the Trinitarian Universalist position, states:

The following are problematic verses for Trinitarian Universalists and which they usually seek to qualify in some way.

The Parable of the Sheep and the Goats
Matthew 25:14–30

Jesus is teaching a principle of Kingdom living: small acts of kindness have eternal value. This is not a teaching about what merits salvation and what merits damnation and it is definitely not a teaching about the eternity of hell. Also, the Greek word 'aion' can be interpreted as 'a long time' as well as 'eternal'. Finally, this passage may not be dealing with personal eschatology at all, but rather with the judgement of Christ on nations based on how they treat his children. On this view, the passage teaches that nations that abuse Christians will be subject to enduring chastisement while those who protect Christians will enjoy enduring life.

Pauline writings
2 Thessalonians 1:9

The phrase 'everlasting destruction' could be translated as 'destruction of the coming age' which makes it a reference to eschatological judgment. The phrase 'and shut out' should be translated as 'that comes from'. Therefore the verse should be read as: 'They will be punished with destruction of the coming age that comes from the presence of the Lord and from the majesty of his power.' The imagery is that of the holiness of God burning away forever the sinful nature of unrepentant man.

Eschaton in Revelation
Revelation 14:11

In view of the overwhelming evidence for Universalism in the Bible, especially in the writings of Paul, this description is hyperbole. Revelation images are metaphorical and no one knows what they really mean.

Some attempts to explain the passage note the ancient uses of burning sulfur for ritual purification and even medicinal therapy, that the Greek word for 'torment' -basanazo- refers to applying a touchstone to determine the presence of gold, and that the Greek word for sulfur 'theoin' is rooted in the Greek 'theos' for 'god'. Thus, the passage could be paraphrased that those who worship the Beast would be tested, tried, even purged and healed through the 'burning sulfur' of the Divine Presence, and that such an ordeal will endure for aions of anions, however long is needed for their restoration.

Revelation 19:3

This refers to the whore of Babylon which is a metaphor for Corinthian political systems and/or economic policies. It is not a reference to the eternal suffering of people.

In Revelation, the kings of the earth are depicted as in league with the Whore of Babylon, which is probably symbolic of corrupt political and/or socioeconomic systems, and they are drunk on the maddening wine of her adulteries. They weep and mourn when she is finally thrown into the Lake of Fire. Then they gather on the plains of Megiddo with the Beast to fight the 'King of kings and Lord of lords' and the armies of heaven in the final battle, Armageddon. They are defeated and the Beast and his False Prophet are thrown into the Lake of Fire. Those who followed them are slain with 'the sword that came out of the mouth' of the Word of God which is probably symbolic of the Gospel or Truth. But in the last scene in New Jerusalem, where the gates are ever open, where the leaves of the trees are for the healing of the nations, the kings of the earth are expected to enter, bringing their splendor with them.

Romans 9, to Calvinism, teaches that some people are natural objects of God's wrath, created and prepared for the purpose of being destroyed. Judas was predestined to be the Son of Perdition, the one prophesied to betray Jesus. It is written that 'It would be better for him if he had not been born' (despite the fact that, without Judas' betrayal there would have been no crucifixion, no resurrection and therefore no salvation). God foreknew all those he would save and that some people are destined for eternal damnation. Also, Corinthians to Calvinism, justice requires that sins against an infinite, holy God merit eternal punishment, especially for those who reject his gift of salvation. God is love and also holy. Thirdly, Calvinists would contend that nowhere in the bible does it even hint at the possibility of post-mortem salvation. After death comes judgment.

Trinitarian Universalists might answer that, if all are created totally lost in sin, it would therefore not be logical or (more importantly) just for God, the epitome of justice himself, to hold them accountable for their actions or liable for their state of being without providing them a way to find redemption, and this could be said even of a being that is not all-merciful and all-loving, as God is. Romans 9 deals with God's hidden will to choose some to salvation in this life (the elect) and pass others, called reprobates, by in this life. That is not the final word God speaks to those individuals he passes by. Jesus said, as he was dying on the cross, 'Father forgive them for they know not what they do.' He also promised 'I, if I be lifted up from the earth, will draw (or, literally, 'drag' in the Greek) all men unto me.' Surely these global statements cover all of humanity.

F.W. Farrar offers this possible interpretation to Jesus' remarks regarding Judas. When Jesus said, 'it would be better for him if he had not been born,' the 'him' was referring to the Son of Man (Jesus) and the 'he' to Judas. Thus he meant that it would have been better for the Son of Man if Judas had not been born. Another view is that although everyone else is to be saved, perhaps Judas will be punished and then annihilated. At any rate the passage does not disprove universalism and certainly does not prove eternal torment.

Pointing to God's eternality is not a satisfactory explanation as to why a temporal sin logically entails unending punishment, though it may be for that reason eternally grave. God's attributes can never conflict with one another, lest God be an imperfect being who is subject to internal strife. God's mercy can never violate his justice, as if God's Love pushes him in one direction whereas his holiness pushes him in another. Universalism brings all his attributes into harmony by pointing out the way in which they describe the one single will of God. The early twentieth century theologian Paul Tillich described this relationship between God's justice and mercy as 'creative justice' and as 'the strange work of love' in Love, Power, and Justice.

His grace, which He freely bestowed on us in the Beloved.' Ephesians 1:4–6Creative justice refers to justice under the principle of agape, or unambiguous and unconditional love. Because it drives towards the reunion of the separated (eros) unconditionally (agape), it makes amends with s/he whom is separated by severing from their personal center that which entrenches the separation (i.e. 'the strange work'). This ultimately entails being faced with the Law, or the unconditionality of the moral imperative, and recognizing the need for reconciliation and forgiveness. This 'destructive' work of love is always for the sake of building up love's object as and into a subject. Gestalt therapy and psychotherapy are modern examples of love doing this strange work: the process is painful and entails major reform, but health and well-being are its intention. Martin Luther said 'the love of God creates its own object.'

From the point of view of Trinitarian Universalism the following questions could be asked of more 'orthodox' believers: If there is no hint of post-mortem salvation in the Bible, then why does Paul refer to people being baptized for the dead? Why did Jesus preach to those in hell? Why did the majority of church fathers, including Augustine and Luther, believe in the possibility of post-mortem salvation?

Arminian objections

Arminianism holds that God will not abrogate humanity's free will because love must be chosen, not forced, and that some people will choose alienation from God over consummation, and so God has 'graciously' provided a place for them to exist. C.S. Lewis speculated, through literary allegory, that hell is locked from within but few will leave because over a lifetime and through the coming ages, they will become more and more at home in hell.

A Trinitarian Universalist believer might counter that for God to allow his misguided and confused children to suffer eternal separation from him is the very opposite of grace, runs counter to his loving and sovereign nature, and would compare unfavorably to the attitude and behavior of even average human parents toward their children. The Bible seems to teach that those who believe do so because God caused them to believe, not by any freedom of choice of their own (Ephesians 2:8–10), and they might cite the following in support their answer:

He choose us in Him before the foundation of the world, that we would be holy and blameless before Him. In love He predestined us to adoption as sons through Jesus Christ to Himself, according to the kind intention of His will, to the praise of the glory of God.

For He says to Moses, 'I will have mercy on whom I have mercy, and I will have compassion on whom I have compassion.' So then it {does} not {depend} on the man who wills or the man who runs, but on God who has mercy.' Romans 9:15–16 (See also: John 15:16, Philippians 1:29, Ephesians 1:11)

Also, the Bible in several places refers to freedom being only for those freed through Christ, and that those who are not in Christ are in darkness under the dominion of Satan (Acts 26:18), and are slaves to sin (John 8:34). Therefore, it would make no sense to maintain that someone can have the 'freedom' to 'reject God'—it is only by sin that people reject God. Those in sin are slaves to sin and Satan, and therefore it is only God who can, by his grace, release them from that bondage and make them able to believe:

'The Lord's bond-servant must not be quarrelsome, but be kind to all, able to teach, patient when wronged, with gentleness correcting those who are in opposition, if perhaps God may grant them repentance leading to the knowledge of the truth, and they may come to their senses {and escape} from the snare of the devil, having been held captive by him to do his will.'

Furthermore, the idea that God wills us to have real love, and that therefore the love cannot be forced upon us, is not to say that, therefore, the only other alternative is absolute and total freedom, even freedom to condemn ourselves. A good parent would certainly allow their son or daughter to develop into their own genuine person, making free choices. That doesn't mean, however, that the parent's earnest desire for authenticity in their child's life, based on the child making real, honest, personal choices, would therefore lead them to not intervene if the child were about to jump in front of a moving train, or take a fatal dose of sleeping pills. To say that God either gives us absolute and total freedom to accept or reject him, or else we are mindless robots or marionettes is a false dichotomy. It also conveniently ignores the blatant fact that almost nothing in our life is under our control, from when and where we are born, to our economic status, to what sorts of beliefs we are taught and raised with—all of which have a bearing on our decision to accept or reject Him. No matter how much we would like to pretend otherwise, the decision to have faith in Christ is not as much 'free will' as it is the enormously personal culmination of all the circumstances of our lives, and therefore enormously influenced by the myriad external, uncontrollable factors that have shaped our hearts and minds.

In the following section I will share information that may possibly lead to questions requiring an answer. I will also directly ask some questions needing to be answered by the Trinitarian:

- **Theological Dictionary of the New Testament:**

> In many passages, of course, the use is rhetorical, but in the general context even these instances imply the total claim of God and his word.

1. In the first place the universal God has chosen Israel.
    a. Israel must keep all the law, the cultic legislation applies to all the people, and the expiatory rites take away all guilt.
    b. All who disobey, and all Israel's foes, fall under God's wrath.
    c. Yet Israel's history is a revelation to all peoples.
        i. God is the one God over all kingdoms, and his judgments extend to the whole world.
        ii. God is the Savior in all troubles, all his ways are mercy and truth, his wrath smites all the wicked, but his salvation is for all believers.
        iii. He knows and sees all things, tries all hearts, and can do all things.
        iv. Even when a particularism of salvation is present, the belief in God's omnipotence, and in the universal validity of his word and claim, is never lost.
        v. A sense of the universal reach of his loving purpose comes out even in passages relating primarily to Israel (cf. 1 Kings 8:37ff.).

- What is done with the universal wrath of God that "smites the wicked?"
- The Trinitarian claims that all history prior to the death of Christ is unrelated to us today – it may be true, or allegorical. Why then do they apply the universality of His "reach of his loving purpose [coming] out even in passages relating primarily to Israel"?

> *Matthew 6:12 and forgive us our sins, as we have forgiven those who sin against us. 13 And don't let us yield to temptation, but rescue us from the evil one. 14 If you forgive those who sin against you, your heavenly Father will forgive you. 15 But if you refuse to forgive others, your Father will not forgive your sins. (NLT)*

- If we have already been forgiven, then how/why is our personal forgiveness tied to our forgiveness of others?
- If we are born forgiven, what power does the "evil one" have from which we need to be rescued?

> *Matthew 25:46 "And they will go away into eternal punishment, but the righteous will go into eternal life." (NLT)*

Will not eternal punishment last as long as eternal salvation?

If one can move from eternal punishment (after death) into eternal righteousness, then can one change from eternal righteousness into eternal punishment?

> *Hebrews 12:14 - Work at living in peace with everyone, and work at living a holy life, for those who are not holy will not see the Lord. (NLT)*

- If one dies while unholy, (not conformed / not saved), how can they receive a second chance when God has said they "will not" see the Lord?
- If we (and all living) have a second chance even after death, could / will the demons and Satan also be given a second chance?

> *Jude 14 Enoch, who lived in the seventh generation after Adam, prophesied about these people. He said, 'Listen! The Lord is coming with countless thousands of his holy ones 15 to execute judgment on the people of the world. He will convict every person of all the ungodly things they have done and for all the insults that ungodly sinners have spoken against him.' 16 These people are grumblers and complainers, living only to satisfy their desires. They brag loudly about themselves, and they flatter others to get what they want. (NLT)*

- Since Trinitarians believe we are already His child whether we know it or not, how and why will God convict and execute judgment on the people of the world?

- And, how and why will He convict us of our ungodly things?

> *John 16:7 But in fact, it is best for you that I go away, because if I don't, the Advocate won't come. If I do go away, then I will send him to you. 8 And when he comes, he will convict the world of its sin, and of God's righteousness, and of the coming judgment. 9 The world's sin is that it refuses to believe in me. 10 Righteousness is available because I go to the Father, and you will see me no more. 11 Judgment will come because the ruler of this world has already been judged. (NLT)*

- How can the Holy Spirit convict the world of its sin when we have already been separated from it from the foundation of the world?
- What judgment is coming if all are forgiven?

> *Ephesians 2:1 Once you were dead because of your disobedience and your many sins. 2 You used to live in sin, just like the rest of the world, obeying the devil—the commander of the powers in the unseen world. He is the spirit at work in the hearts of those who refuse to obey God. 3 All of us used to live that way, following the passionate desires and inclinations of our sinful nature. By our very nature we were subject to God's anger, just like everyone else. 4 But God is so rich in mercy, and he loved us so much, 5 that even though we were dead because of our sins, he gave us life when he raised Christ from the dead. (It is only by God's*

grace that you have been saved!) 6 For he raised us from the dead along with Christ and seated us with him in the heavenly realms because we are united with Christ Jesus. 7 So God can point to us in all future ages as examples of the incredible wealth of his grace and kindness toward us, as shown in all he has done for us who are united with Christ Jesus. 8 God saved you by his grace when you believed. And you can't take credit for this; it is a gift from God. (NLT)

- How can the devil be at work in the hearts of those refusing to obey when they are eternally forgiven and are God's child since before birth?

- Does not there seem to be a distinction between us who have come to salvation and those who haven't, since in verse three it states, "all of us used to live that way." We were subject, just like everyone else.

- By our very nature, how can we be subject to God's anger? How can this be if we are already forgiven?

Colossians 2:13 Then God made you alive with Christ, for he forgave all our sins. (NLT)

- With statements like, "you were," and "then God made, "how can there be a past tense of our being dead when we have been made alive since Christ hung on the cross?

- If we have been forgiven from the foundation of the world, then how can we be dead because of our sin?

  > Col 1:21 This includes you who were once far away from God. You were his enemies, separated from him by your evil thoughts and actions. 22 Yet now he has reconciled you to himself through the death of Christ in his physical body. As a result, he has brought you into his own presence, and you are holy and blameless as you stand before him without a single fault (NLT)

- How can our sins already be forgiven while not yet being appropriated by faith?
- How can I be God's enemy at the same time I am already His child?

  > Matthew 3:7 But when he saw many Pharisees and Sadducees coming to watch him baptize, he denounced them. 'You brood of snakes!' he exclaimed. 'Who warned you to flee God's coming wrath? 8 Prove by the way you live that you have repented of your sins and turned to God. 9 Don't just say to each other, 'We're safe, for we are descendants of Abraham.' That means nothing, for I tell you, God can create children of Abraham from these very stones. 10 Even now the ax of God's judgment is poised, ready to sever the roots of the trees. Yes, every tree that does not produce good fruit will be chopped down and thrown into the fire. (NLT)

- Why should we prove, by the way we live, that we have repented? If it is already a completed action, there is nothing to prove.
- What wrath of God is coming, and what ax of God's judgment?
- Can the tree that has been chopped down and cast into the fire be replanted to produce fruit? If not, since this is an allegory, what does that say about the Trinitarian belief that we have other chances after death?

> *Mark 11:25 But when you are praying, first forgive anyone you are holding a grudge against, so that your Father in heaven will forgive your sins, too.' (NLT)*

- How can forgiveness be conditioned on our forgiveness of others?
- How can it be ongoing if it is already a completed action?

> *1 Corinthians 11:27 So anyone who eats this bread or drinks this cup of the Lord unworthily is guilty of sinning against the body and blood of the Lord. 28 That is why you should examine yourself before eating the bread and drinking the cup. 29 For if you eat the bread or drink the cup without honoring the body of Christ, you are eating and drinking God's judgment upon yourself. 30 That is why many of you are weak and sick and some have even died. (NLT)*

- How can your actions cause God's judgment?

- Does not this indicate a punishment from God for actions (sins) while living in this world?

  Hebrews 10:26 Dear friends, if we deliberately continue sinning after we have received knowledge of the truth, there is no longer any sacrifice that will cover these sins. 27 There is only the terrible expectation of God's judgment and the raging fire that will consume his enemies. 28 For anyone who refused to obey the law of Moses was put to death without mercy on the testimony of two or three witnesses. 29 Just think how much worse the punishment will be for those who have trampled on the Son of God, and have treated the blood of the covenant, which made us holy, as if it were common and unholy, and have insulted and disdained the Holy Spirit who brings God's mercy to us. (NLT)

- Is it possible in the Trinitarian theology for sinful actions to cause the forgiveness to end? If so, when and how?
- How can we invite a worse punishment by our actions?
- And, how can there be a worse punishment when all of our sin, wickedness, wrongdoing, or debt has already been placed on Christ and forgiven?

  James 4:4 You adulterers! Don't you realize that friendship with the world makes you an enemy of God? I say it again: If you want to be a friend of the world, you make yourself an enemy of God. 5 What do you think the Scriptures mean when they say that the spirit God has placed within us is filled with envy? 6 But he gives us even more grace to stand against such evil desires. As the Scriptures say, 'God opposes the proud but favors the humble.' 7 So humble yourselves before God. Resist the devil, and he will flee from you. 8 Come close to God, and God will come close to you. Wash your hands, you sinners; purify your hearts, for your loyalty is divided between God and the world. (NLT)

- How can anyone be an enemy of God?
- How could God oppose some while favoring others?
- Is it possible for the god of the Trinitarian to be close to some and not to others?

James 5:14 Are any of you sick? You should call for the elders of the church to come and pray over you, anointing you with oil in the name of the Lord. 15 Such a prayer offered in faith will heal the sick, and the Lord will make you well. And if you have committed any sins, you will be forgiven. (NLT)

- "Will be" forgiven? Why not "already" as an accomplished fact?

James 5:16 Confess your sins to each other and pray for each other so that you may be healed. The earnest prayer of a righteous person has

great power and produces wonderful results.
(NLT)

- Why confess what has already been forgiven?

  Hebrews 12:6 For the Lord disciplines those he
  loves, and he punishes each one he accepts as his
  child.' 7 As you endure this divine discipline,
  remember that God is treating you as his own
  children. Who ever heard of a child who is
  never disciplined by its father? 8 If God doesn't
  discipline you as he does all of his children, it
  means that you are illegitimate and are not
  really his children at all. (NLT)

- What is the purpose of God's discipline? And
  how could God punish those who are already
  righteous?
- Would this punishment and discipline indicate
  any aspect of God's wrath, since it is activated
  by our sin?

  Proverbs 28:13 People who conceal their sins
  will not prosper, but if they confess and turn
  from them, they will receive mercy. (NLT)

- Is mercy tied to turning and confessing?

  Act 2:38… Peter replied, 'Each of you must
  repent of your sins, turn to God, and be
  baptized in the name of Jesus Christ to show
  that you have received forgiveness for your sins.
  Then you will receive the gift of the Holy Spirit.
  (NLT)

- If repentance is wrong after salvation, why is it needed for salvation? Would not that be an effort (work) beyond what Christ has already done?

> *Ephesians 5:5 You can be sure that no immoral, impure, or greedy person will inherit the Kingdom of Christ and of God. For a greedy person is an idolater, worshiping the things of this world. 6 Don't be fooled by those who try to excuse these sins, for the anger of God will fall on all who disobey him. (NLT)*

- Can you be sure – no immoral, impure, or greedy person will inherit the Kingdom?
- If we are eternally "pre" forgiven, how could we be categorized in these groupings?
- Regarding God's "anger" falling on all, how can God have anger towards us and what is there for Him to be angry about if it is already dealt with by Christ on our behalf?

> *Ephesians 5:10 Carefully determine what pleases the Lord. 11 Take no part in the worthless deeds of evil and darkness; instead, expose them. 12 It is shameful even to talk about the things that ungodly people do in secret. 13 But their evil intentions will be exposed when the light shines on them, 14 for the light makes everything visible. This is why it is said, "Awake, O sleeper, rise up from the dead, and Christ will give you light." (NLT)*

- Is it possible for people to be "ungodly" when they are His child from before birth "whether they realize it or not"?

  1 Corinthians 14:24 But if all of you are prophesying, and unbelievers or people who don't understand these things come into your meeting, they will be convicted of sin and judged by what you say. (NLT)

- How / why be judged when they were born forgiven?

  1 Timothy5:20 Those who sin should be reprimanded in front of the whole church; this will serve as a strong warning to others.

- For what would they be reprimanded?

  2 Timothy 4:2 Preach the word of God. Be prepared, whether the time is favorable or not. Patiently correct, rebuke, and encourage your people with good teaching. (NLT)

- Why correct, rebuke people?

  Hebrews 12:7 If God doesn't discipline you as he does all of his children, it means that you are illegitimate and are not really his children at all. 9 Since we respected our earthly fathers who disciplined us, shouldn't we submit even more to the discipline of the Father of our spirits, and live forever? (NLT)

- Why would God discipline us?

- How can I "not really [be] his child at all?"

  Revelation 3:19 I correct and discipline everyone I love. So be diligent and turn from your indifference. (NLT)

- Why would God correct and discipline us when all correction and punishment for our sins has been placed on Christ and removed from us?

  2 Corinthians 7:8 I am not sorry that I sent that severe letter to you, though I was sorry at first, for I know it was painful to you for a little while. 9 Now I am glad I sent it, not because it hurt you, but because the pain caused you to repent and change your ways. It was the kind of sorrow God wants his people to have, so you were not harmed by us in any way. 10 For the kind of sorrow God wants us to experience leads us away from sin and results in salvation. There's no regret for that kind of sorrow. But worldly sorrow, which lacks repentance, results in spiritual death. (NLT)

- Can pain cause them to repent and change their ways? What is this pain and from where does it come?
- Can God want us to have sorrow when all He desires is for us to agree and thank Him for what we already have?

  2 Corinthians 7:11 Just see what this godly sorrow produced in you! Such earnestness, such concern to clear yourselves, such indignation, such alarm, such longing to see me, such zeal, and such a readiness to punish wrong. You showed that you have done everything necessary to make things right. (NLT)

- Isn't this more than agreeing with God? It implies we must do something to make things right. But how, if all things have been made right by and through Christ for us?

Romans 6:20 When you were slaves to sin, you were free from the obligation to do right. 21 And what was the result? You are now ashamed of the things you used to do, things that end in eternal doom. 22 But now you are free from the power of sin and have become slaves of God. Now you do those things that lead to holiness and result in eternal life. (NLT)

- Why exhort to live a certain way that will lead to sanctification if you are already sanctified?
- What things can we do that "result in eternal life?"

Philippians 3:12 I don't mean to say that I have already achieved these things or that I have already reached perfection. But I press on to possess that perfection for which Christ Jesus first possessed me. (NLT)

- Has not obtained? How can that be if he already has been?

Francis Chan: (Erasing Hell...)

... I said at the beginning that the one thing all Christian Universalists agree upon is that after death there will be another chance (or an endless string of chances) to choose Jesus.

No passage in the Bible says that there will be a second chance after death to turn to Jesus...

... One Christian Universalist admits this... 'Clearly my interpretation is underdetermined by the texts... I am not so much exegeting the text as trying to draw out the logic of New Testament theology as I understand it and its implications for these texts. In the process I may be offering ways of reading the texts that go beyond what their authors had in mind.' MacDonald, The Evangelical Universalist, 140.

When once the master of the house has risen and shut the door, and you begin to stand and knock at the door, saying, 'Lord, open to us,' then he will answer you, 'I do not know where you come from... Depart from me, all you workers of evil!' In that place there will be weeping and gnashing of teeth, when you see Abraham and Isaac and Jacob and all the prophets in the kingdom of God but you yourselves cast out.' (Luke 13:25-28)

This passage 'gives no hint whatever that the door will remain permanently open.' Marshall, 'The New Testament Does Not Teach Universal Salvation,' 59. If Jesus believed in second chances for those who reject Him in the life, then this parable is dangerously misleading."

Genesis 3:22 Then the Lord God said, "Look, the human beings have become like us, knowing both good and evil. What if they reach out, take fruit from the tree of life, and eat it? Then they will live forever!" 23 So the Lord God banished them from the Garden of Eden, and he sent Adam out to cultivate the ground from which he had been made. 24 After sending them out, the Lord God stationed mighty cherubim to the east of the Garden of Eden. And he placed a flaming sword that flashed back and forth to guard the way to the tree of life. (NLT)

- If He has already given to everyone eternal life, then why banish them from the tree of life so that they cannot "live forever"?
- If God has forgiven all, and if His works are not based on anger, retribution, or punishment, but are actually works of pure love, and only for the purpose of drawing all men, then…
- What of the individuals (all ages – young and old) being destroyed in the flood?
- Sodom and Gomorrah (all ages – young and old) being destroyed?
- First Born Egyptian male children killed by death angel?
- Achan and family (including children and animals) killed at God's direction?
- What of Agag and Amalikites (1 Samuel 15) Saul commanded by God to kill everyone, small and great, pregnant, young and old, and all animals to be killed?

- What of the Mount of Cursing and Blessings from God to Israel with negative responses from God to those who did not follow God's command?

  "A condemned man on death row might have someone offer to and actually die in his place. But unless the man believes this outrageous act on his behalf has actually been accomplished he will languish in jail until his own execution is at hand. So the condemned sinner must believe what Christ has accomplished for him or he will never enjoy its benefits." (Free Grace Soteriology, David R. Anderson)

  In the OT, God tended to deal with salvation through nations more than individuals (dealing with groups not personally) ibid

- If all are "already God's children whether they know it or not," then how could God pronounce a "curse" on anyone for any reason?

  Galatians 1:8 Let God's curse fall on anyone, including us or even an angel from heaven, who preaches a different kind of Good News than the one we preached to you. 9 I say again what we have said before: If anyone preaches any other Good News than the one you welcomed, let that person be cursed. (NLT)

- How can God curse anyone?

- If this verse is accurate, (and it is), then what does that say about those who change and make God's Good New different?
- How do the Trinitarians answer these verses that declare people righteous because of **their** faith, not the faith **of Jesus** as the Trinitarian believe?

> *Galatians 3:8 What's more, the Scriptures looked forward to this time when God would declare the Gentiles to be righteous* **because of their faith**. *God proclaimed this good news to Abraham long ago when he said, "All nations will be blessed through you." 9 So all who put their faith in Christ share the same blessing Abraham received because of his faith.*

> *Romans 4:5 But people are counted as righteous, not because of their work, but* **because of their own personal faith** *in God who forgives sinners.*

> *Romans 8:9 ... (And remember that those who do not have the Spirit of Christ living in them do not belong to him at all. (NLT)*

- At what point is someone indwelt by the Holy Spirit?
- If they are "Already His children whether they know it or not...." If they are born forgiven and His child, then what does Romans 8:9 mean?
- Are they, like John the Baptist, indwelt while in the womb?

In John chapter three Christ explains to Nicodemus that there are two births:

a. The first is physical and places you into the physical family of humanity (Adam).
b. The second is spiritual and places you into the spiritual family of God (Second Adam).
c. The first birth is:
    i.   Given by God at the moment of creation in the womb.
    ii. Places you into mankind's kingdom of the flesh.
    iii. The one being given life has no choice in conception.
    iv. But once born he can choose to end life by personal decision.
d. The second birth is:
    i.   Offered by God from eternity past.
    ii. Places you into God's spiritual kingdom.
    iii. The one receiving the offer has a choice in reception.
    iv. Once accepted it cannot end by personal choice.
    v.   Once final rejection is made (at death) it cannot be accepted at a later time.

Every person born into the kingdom of man's flesh is born a sinner. And 'all' (every one, in total, no exceptions) die in (because) Adam (Romans 5:12-15).

Every person (everyone, in total, no exception) born into the kingdom of God's Spirit is born into that kingdom forgiven and just like Christ (1 John 4:17; Romans 5:15-17). This would not include those not born into that kingdom.

(See "Barnes Notes" #4, a, b, c.)

Result: all in Adam die. All in Christ live.

Everyone (all) who are part of humanity die.

Universally applied to those who are part of the fleshly Adam's family.

Everyone (all) who are *in* Christ are made alive / forgiven.

i. Universally applied to those who are part of the spiritual Adam's family.

Determined by the birth… born into Adam's family, born into Christ's.

"Clark Whitten states that Luther and Calvin followed by the Protestant church ever since, taught a doctrine of 'saved by grace but perfected by human effort,' an approach that has produced 'a church that is judgmental, angry, hopeless, helpless, dependent, fearful, uninspired, ineffective and perpetually spiritually immature." Michael Brown, Hyper Grace, Exposing the Dangers

In conversation with some holding to the Trinitarian view who describe their position as a "hopeful universalist", I have been told that God will continue to pursue the individual even after they have entered eternity. This pursuit will continue until the person finally realizes what God's love has provided and with thanksgiving simply accept the gift.

- On what biblical basis, anywhere in Scripture, is it shown that God pursues a soul even after death giving them opportunity to change his choice and become thankful for God's grace and gift?

- If, by chance, their "proof text" is the portion of Scripture used of Christ preaching to the souls in hades, should one Scripture be used to develop a questionable belief when it is not augmented by (many) other Scripture indicating the same "truth"?

- Is this a prime example of what Charles Hodge described when he said, "Speculation assumes… certain principles, and from them undertakes to determine what is and what must be. It decides on all truth, or determines on what is true from the laws of the mind, or from the axioms involved in the constitution of the thinking principle within us… 'Scripture serves as an aid to natural theology… consequently the philosopher is bound not to invent but to demonstrate.'"? If so, please give biblical demonstration.

I have been told by Trinitarians that the only literal hell is found in life with its pains while here on earth. They believe that Heaven and hell exist congruently with those in Heaven enjoying the benefits of God's grace, while those not yet accepting of His grace are being tormented by the realization of being outside God's grace while not experiencing the benefits.

- Once again, where is this found in Scripture? Is this another example of the Speculative method of applied theology (Dr. Hodge, Systematic Theology)?

> *John 5:28 Don't be so surprised! Indeed, the time is coming when all the dead in their graves will hear the voice of God's Son, 29 and they will rise again. Those who have done good will rise to experience eternal life, and those who have continued in evil will rise to experience judgment. (NLT)*

- How can they be raised to face judgment and how can that judgment be based on their evil actions?

> *John 3:18 "There is no judgment against anyone who believes in him. But anyone who does not believe in him has already been judged for not believing in God's one and only Son. 19 And the judgment is based on this fact: God's light came into the world, but people loved the darkness more than the light, for their actions were evil. 20 All who do evil hate the light and refuse to go near it for fear their sins will be exposed. (NLT)*

- It seems that judgment is based on not believing. And the truth they did not believe was Jesus is the light of the world. How can this be when they already possess forgiveness and acceptance through (because / by) Jesus?

> *Matthew 25:44 "Then they will reply, 'Lord, when did we ever see you hungry or thirsty or a stranger or naked or sick or in prison, and not help you?' 45 "And he will answer, 'I tell you the truth, when you refused to help the least of*

these my brothers and sisters, you were refusing to help me.' 46 "And they will go away into eternal punishment, but the righteous will go into eternal life." (NLT)

- The word "eternal" is the same in both examples, (eternal punishment and eternal life). Does this imply that one can give back eternal life?
- And is it even possible since he will not receive eternal punishment because God is eternally pursuing him in eternity?

  2 Thessalonians 1:7 ... He will come with his mighty angels, 8 in flaming fire, bringing judgment on those who don't know God and on those who refuse to obey the Good News of our Lord Jesus. 9 They will be punished with eternal destruction, forever separated from the Lord and from his glorious power. (NLT)

- What judgment will be given to those who don't know God? In fact, what judgment even exists since everything has already been inflicted on Christ for us?

  1 Peter 3:20 those who disobeyed God long ago when God waited patiently while Noah was building his boat. Only eight people were saved from drowning in that terrible flood. (NLT)

- Did God punish humanity (except for the eight) for their sin by drowning?
- Why?

- What is your response to Barnes Commentary (1 Timothy 4:9) when he writes:

  "[Who is the Savior of all men] This must be understood as denoting that he is the Savior of all people in some sense which differs from what is immediately affirmed - "especially of those that believe." There is something pertaining to "them" in regard to salvation which does not pertain to "all men." It cannot mean that he brings all people to heaven, "especially" those who believe-for this would be nonsense. And if he brings all people actually to heaven, how can it be "especially" true that he does this in regard to those who believe? ...

  "Does it mean that he saves others 'without' believing? But this would be contrary to the uniform doctrine of the Scriptures; see Mark 16:16. When, therefore, it is said that he 'is the Savior of 'all' people, 'especially' of those who believe,' it must mean that there is a sense in which it is true that he may be called the Savior of all people, while, at the same time, it is 'actually' true that those only are saved who believe."?

- How do you explain the "especially" question of Barnes?
- Does that then mean that God saves some who do not believe?
- *Or, should it be understood as Jamieson, Fausset, and Brown Commentary says, "He is the Savior of all sufficiently and potentially (1 Timothy 1:15); and of believers alone efficiently and effectively."?*

- And what of Adam Clarke's comments regarding Matthew 25:46 dealing with the word 'eternal'?

  But some are of opinion that this punishment shall have an end: this is as likely as that the glory of the righteous shall have an end: for the same word is used to express the duration of the punishment, "kolasin aioonion," as is used to express the duration of the state of glory: "zooeen aioonion."

- How are we to understand Barnes comments when dealing with "our faith" being required in salvation and not the "faith of" Jesus?

  "But the Holy Spirit does not 'repent' for us. It is our 'own mind' that repents; our own heart that feels; our own eyes that weep—and without this there can be no true repentance. No one can repent for another; and God neither can nor ought to repent; for us. He has done no wrong, and if repentance is ever exercised, therefore, it must be exercised by our own minds."

I pray that this exercise brings questions in every reader's mind and furthermore that they enjoy the search for answers. By using Dr. Hodge's Inductive Method of theological study, I am confident the truth will be evident.

Opinions of the Sages

Our Bible is the foundation of truth. What God intends for us to know about Him and His universe, both practically and doctrinally, will be found in those sixty-six books. It has been said that if someone was to write all there is to know about God, the books would fill the universe and then some. In other words, we know very little about God – He is eternal. But what we can know about Him is found in the Bible.

On the following pages is a study of each of the verses used in the previous pages by the Trinitarians as proof of their belief. I searched the minds and wisdom of the theologians and the following pages are what I found.

I must admit that I am tempted to stop along the way and yell, "That's right! You go girl!" But I am avoiding that and also ask for forgiveness for the "You go girl!" That's just my humanity hanging out on the pages. I am ask the Holy Spirit to guide into His truth as it relates to the study of this issue and I have included the words of those more learned in the languages and texts.

Readers will find a general theme and response to Origen and those who followed in the Trinitarian way as well as direct quotes with an absence of opinion from me or contemporary Christian leaders, though I have included a quote from Francis Chan.

Titus 2:11 For the grace of God has been revealed, bringing salvation to all people. (NLT)

- **Adam Clarke:**

> *Since God's grace signifies God's favor, any benefit received from him may be termed God's grace. In this place, and in Colossians 1:6, the Gospel, which points out God's infinite mercy to the world, is termed the grace of God; for it is not only a favor of infinite worth in itself, but it announces that greatest gift of God to man, the incarnation and atoning sacrifice of Jesus Christ. Now it cannot be said, except in a very refined and spiritual sense, that this Gospel had then appeared to all men; but it may be well said that it bringeth salvation to all men;*
>
> *From the influences of this spiritual Sun no soul is reprobated any more than from the influences of the natural sun. In both cases, only those who willfully shut their eyes, and hide themselves in darkness, are deprived of the gracious benefit.*

- **Barnes:**

> *...to all men, hath appeared. That is, in the margin, 'the grace which brings salvation to all men has been revealed.'*
>
> *If that which is in the text be adopted, it means that the plan of salvation has been revealed to all classes of men; that is, that it is announced or revealed to all the race that they may be saved;*

- **Bible Knowledge Commentary:**

> *This grace has brought salvation to all men, i.e., it is universally available.*

- **Bible Exposition Commentary:**

> *This salvation is for 'all men' who receive it (see 1 Timothy2:4-6). There is a universal need, and God provided a universal remedy for all who will believe.*

- **Biblical Illustrator:**

> *II. THE UNIVERSALITY OF ITS APPEARANCE.*
>
> *1. Adapted for all.*
>
> *2. Revealed for all.*
>
> *3. To be proclaimed to all.*
>
> *The grace of God, that bringeth salvation hath appeared unto all men'; or, according to the translation in the margin of our Bibles, 'The grace of God, which bringeth salvation to all men, hath appeared'*
>
> *The gospel, then, is described as bringing salvation to all men; that is, as offering to all who accept it free and full remission of sin, through the blood of the Lord Jesus; as opening to all believers the gate of the kingdom of heaven.*
>
> *That grace received rescues from the disastrous effects of sin; heals our inward diseases, and comforts our sorrows; and then we call it mercy.*
>
> *Yes, God's free favor, manifested in the person of His own blessed Son, is designed to produce saving effects upon all. God makes no exception, excludes none. All are not saved. But why not? Not because the grace of God does not bring salvation to every man, but because all men do not receive the gift which the grace of God has brought to them.*
>
> *Before any benefit can accrue from a gift there must be a willingness on the one side to give, and a willingness*

on the other side to receive, and unless there be both of these conditions realized no satisfactory result can ensue.

It brings salvation to all men. It does not follow from that that all men take the salvation which it brings. Notice the underlying theory of a universal need that lies in these words. The grace brings salvation to all men, because all men need that more than anything else.

That they cannot mean every individual of our race. It is matter of fact that many, both in the days of the apostles, and in our own time are, wholly unenlightened by the good news of salvation.

The grace of God appears to all kinds of men. None are excluded from it who do not exclude themselves.

- **IVP Bible Background Commentary:**

    That God's grace had provided (though not automatically effected — cf., e.g., 1:10) salvation for all people ran counter to Jewish exclusivism and previous sentiments of cultural distinctions held by many people in antiquity

- **Jewish NT Commentary:**

    Nevertheless, not everyone is saved because not everyone has committed himself to this grace.

- **Matthew Henry:**

    It hath appeared to all men; not to the Jews only, as the glory of God appeared at Mount Sinai to that particular people, and out of the view of all others; but gospel grace is open to all, and all are invited to come and partake of the benefit of it,

2 Corinthians 5:14 Either way, Christ's love controls us. Since we believe that Christ died for all, we also believe that we have all died to our old life. (NLT)

- **Life Application Commentary:**

> *Jesus died for all because on the cross he — the perfect Son of God — bore the curse that lay on all sinners. Thus, when Christ died on the cross, God saw all sinners, along with their sins, die on the cross (John 3:16-17; Romans 5:8). That is why those who accept this truth and believe in Jesus can receive God's forgiveness for their sin.*

Mark 11:25 But when you are praying, first forgive anyone you are holding a grudge against, so that your Father in heaven will forgive your sins, too. (NLT)

- **Barnes**

> *'Literally' there can be no such transaction between God and us. It must be used figuratively. We have not met the claims of law. We have violated its obligations. We are exposed to its penalty. We are guilty, and God only can forgive, in the same way as none but a 'creditor' can forgive a debtor. The word "debts" here, therefore, means 'sins,' or offences against God-offences which none but God can forgive.*
>
> *The measure by which we may expect forgiveness is that which we use in reference to others*
>
> *This is the invariable rule by which God dispenses pardon He that comes before him unwilling to forgive, harboring dark and revengeful thoughts, how can he expect that God will show him that mercy which he is unwilling to show to others?*

But it was probably intended to refer principally to injuries of character or person which we have received from others. If we cannot from the heart forgive them, we have the assurance that God will never forgive us.

- **Bible Knowledge Commentary**

This is to be done in order that his Father in heaven (the only Marcan occurrence of this phrase, but frequent in Matthew.) may 'also' (kai in Gr.) forgive him his sins (lit., paraptomata, 'trespasses,' only occurrence in Mark), acts that sidestep or deviate from God's truth.

Divine forgiveness toward a believer and a believer's forgiveness toward others are inseparably linked because a bond has been established between the divine Forgiver and the forgiven believer (cf. Matthew 18:21-35). One who has accepted God's forgiveness is expected to forgive others just as God has forgiven him (Ephesians 4:32). If he does not, he forfeits God's forgiveness in his daily life.

- **Life Application Commentary**

God wants us to deal with our 'horizontal' relationships in order to have a clear "vertical" relationship (see also Matthew 5:23-24).

Why would this matter? Because all people are sinners before God. Those who have access to him have it only because of his mercy in forgiving their sins. Believers should not come to God asking for forgiveness or making requests, all the while refusing to forgive others. To do so would be to reveal that they have no appreciation for the mercy they have received. God will not listen to a person with such an attitude.)

Colossians 1: 19 God in all his fullness was pleased to live in Christ, 20 and through him God reconciled everything to himself. He made peace with everything in heaven and on earth by means of Christ's blood on the cross. (NLT)

- **Barnes Notes:**

    (1) It relates only to those things which are in heaven and earth-for those only are specified. Nothing is said of the inhabitants of hell, whether fallen angels, or the spirits of wicked men who are there.

    (2) It cannot mean that all things are actually reconciled-for that never has been true. Multitudes on earth have remained alienated from God, and have lived and died his enemies.

    There was no enemy which it was not fitted to reconcile to God; there was no guilt, now producing alienation, which it could not wash away.

- **Bible Knowledge Commentary:**

    The phrase 'all things' is limited to good angels and redeemed people since only things on earth and things in heaven are mentioned. Things 'under the earth' (Philippians 2:10) are not reconciled.

    It is important to note that people are reconciled to God ('to Himself') not that God is reconciled to people. For mankind has left God and needs to be brought back to Him.

- **Bible Exposition Commentary:**

> The sinner is 'dead in trespasses and sins' (Ephesians 2:1ff), and therefore is unable to do anything to save himself or to please God (Romans 8:8).
>
> If there is to be reconciliation between man and God, the initiative and action must come from God. It is in Christ that God was reconciled to man (2 Corinthians 5:19). But it was not the incarnation of Christ that accomplished this reconciliation, nor was it His example as He lived among men. It was through His death that peace was made between God and man. He 'made peace through the blood of His cross' (Colossians 1:20).
>
> We must not conclude wrongly that universal reconciliation is the same as universal salvation. 'Universalism' is the teaching that all beings, including those who have rejected Jesus Christ, will one day be saved. This was not what Paul believed. 'Universal restorationism' was not a part of Paul's theology, for he definitely taught that sinners needed to believe in Jesus Christ to be saved (2 Thessalonians 1).

- **IVP Bible Background Commentary:**

> The reconciling even of the invisible powers (1:16) refers to their subordination rather than their salvation (2:15),

- **Life Application Commentary:**

> Does this reconciliation of 'all things' mean that everyone will be saved? From other passages, we know that Paul understood salvation to be something accepted or rejected by humans, who are given the choice (for example,

see 2 Thessalonians 1:5-10). The scope of God's reconciliation is universal – it is offered to all people. But reconciliation is accomplished only for those who accept Christ as Savior:

1 Timothy 4:9 This is a trustworthy saying, and everyone should accept it. 10 This is why we work hard and continue to struggle, for our hope is in the living God, who is the Savior of all people and particularly of all believers. (NLT)

- **Adam Clarke:**

  [Who is the Savior of all men] Who has provided salvation for the whole human race, and has freely offered it to them in his word and by his Spirit.

  [Especially of those that believe.] What God intends for ALL, he actually gives to them that believe in Christ, who died for the sins of the world, and tasted death for every man. As all have been purchased by his blood so all may believe; and consequently all may be saved. Those that perish, perish through their own fault.

- **Barnes:**

  [Who is the Savior of all men] This must be understood as denoting that he is the Savior of all people in some sense which differs from what is immediately affirmed – 'especially of those that believe.' There is something pertaining to 'them' in regard to salvation which does not pertain to 'all men.' It cannot mean that he brings all people to heaven, 'especially' those who believe-for this would be nonsense. And if he brings all people actually to heaven, how can it be 'especially' true that he does this in

regard to those who believe? Does it mean that he saves others 'without' believing? But this would be contrary to the uniform doctrine of the Scriptures; see Mark 16:16. When, therefore, it is said that he 'is the Savior of 'all' people, 'especially' of those who believe,' it must mean that there is a sense in which it is true that he may be called the Savior of all people, while, at the same time, it is 'actually' true that those only are saved who believe. This may be true in two respects:

(1) As he is the 'Preserver' of people (Job 7:20), for in this sense he may be said to 'save' them from famine, and war, and peril-keeping them from day to day; compare Psalms 107:28;

(2) As he has 'provided' salvation for all people. He is thus their Savior—and may be called the common Savior of all; that is, he has confined the offer of salvation to no one class of people; he has not limited the atonement to one division of the human race; and he actually saves all who are willing to be saved by him.

[Specially of those that believe] This is evidently designed to limit the previous remark. If it had been left there, it might have been inferred that he would 'actually save' all people. But the apostle held no such doctrine, and he here teaches that salvation is 'actually' limited to those who believe. This is the specialty or the uniqueness in the salvation of those who actually reach heaven, that they are 'believers;' see the notes on Mark 16:16. All people, therefore, do not enter heaven, unless all people have faith. But is this so? What evidence is there that the great mass of mankind die believing on the Son of God?

- **Bible Knowledge Commentary:**

> *Again Paul stated that God is the Savior of 'all men' (cf. 2:2,4,6) since He desires that all be saved and He provided Christ as the ransom (2:6) to make that salvation possible. Yet God is the Savior of those who believe in a special way since only in them has His desire for their salvation come to fruition.*

- **Biblical Illustrator:**

> *And, in the next place, this may be especially applied to that part of God's will, in which His glory is most concerned. In the gospel the honor of God is most of all concerned: men are to be saved by believing the gospel: therefore, we may be confident that God will help them in all that relates to the success of the gospel: 'He is the Savior especially of them that believe.*

- **Jamieson, Fausset, and Brown:**

> *He is the Savior of all sufficiently and potentially (1 Timothy1:15); of believers alone efficiently and effectually.*

Hebrews 2:9 What we do see is Jesus, who was given a position 'a little lower than the angels'; and because he suffered death for us, he is now 'crowned with glory and honor.' Yes, by God's grace, Jesus tasted death for everyone. (NLT)

- **Adam Clarke:**

> *In consequence of the fall of Adam, the whole human race became sinful in their natures and in their practice added transgression to sinfulness of disposition,*

and thus became exposed to endless perdition. To redeem them Jesus Christ took on him the nature of man, and suffered the penalty due to their sins.

- **Barnes:**

  [For every man] For all - Huper pantos - for each and all-whether Jew or Gentile, bond or free, high or low, elect or non-elect. How could words affirm more clearly that the atonement made by the Lord Jesus was unlimited in its nature and design? How can we express that idea in more clear or intelligible language? That this refers to the atonement is evident-for it says that he 'tasted death' for them. The friends of the doctrine of general atonement do not desire any other than Scripture language in which to express their belief. It expresses it exactly-without any need of modification or explanation. The advocates of the doctrine of limited atonement CANNOT thus use Scripture language to express their belief. They cannot incorporate it with their creeds that the Lord Jesus 'tasted death FOR EVERY MAN.' They are compelled to modify it, to limit it, to explain it, in order to present error and misconception. But that system CANNOT be true which requires people to shape and modify the plain language of the Bible in order to keep people from error! Compare the notes at 2 Corinthians 5:14, where this point is considered at length.

- **Bible Knowledge Commentary:**

  The focus of the statement despite its reference to Jesus' present glory, is on the fact that He became a man in order to die.

- **Jamieson, Fausett, and Brown:**

    The reading of Origen, 'That He without (chooris for chariti) God' (laying aside His divinity: or, for every being except God; or perhaps 'apart from God,' forsaken, as the sin-bearer, by the Father on the cross), is not supported by manuscripts. The 'that,' etc. is connected with 'crowned with glory,' etc. His exaltation after sufferings is the perfecting of His work (Hebrews 2:10) for us: from it flows the result that His tasting of death is available in behalf of every man. He is crowned as the Head of our common humanity, presenting His blood as the all-prevailing plea for us. This coronation above makes His death applicable for every individual man (singular: not merely 'for all men')

- **Life Application Commentary:**

    'Tasted' means to 'come to know, to experience.' Jesus lived and died physically. He did not experience a 'lesser' death than any other human. Only Jesus lived a perfect life and was the necessary sacrifice for sin so that sinful humanity could fulfill the words of Psalms 8, to finally fulfill God's plan. Jesus died 'for everyone in all the world,' but not everyone will be saved. The only way for people to be saved and to receive God's rewards is to 'believe in the Lord Jesus' (Acts 16:31 NIV).

1 John 2:2 He himself is the sacrifice that atones for our sins—and not only our sins but the sins of all the world. (NLT)

- **Adam Clarke:**

> *[And not for ours only] It is not for us apostles that he has died, nor exclusively for the Jewish people, but peri holou tou kosmou, for the whole world, Gentiles as well as Jews, all the descendants of Adam. The apostle does not say that he died for any select part of the inhabitants of the earth, or for some out of every nation, tribe, or kindred; but for ALL MANKIND: and the attempt to limit this is a violent outrage against God and his word.*
>
> *From these verses we learn that a poor backslider need not despair of again finding mercy; this passage holds out sufficient encouragement for his hope. There is scarcely another such in the Bible; and why! That sinners might not presume on the mercy of God. And why this one! That no backslider might utterly despair. Here, then, is a guard against presumption on the one hand, and despondency on the other.*

- **Barnes:**

> *[And not for our's only] Not only for the sins of us who are Christians, for the apostle was writing to such. The idea which he intends to convey seems to be, that when we come before God we should take the most liberal and large views of the atonement; we should feel that the most ample provision has been made for our pardon, and that in no respect is there any limit as to the sufficiency of that work to remove all sin. It is sufficient for us; sufficient for all the world.*
>
> *[But also for the sins of the whole world] The phrase 'the sins of' is not in the original, but is not improperly supplied, for the connection demands it. This is one of the expressions occurring in the New Testament which*

demonstrate that the atonement was made for all people, and which cannot be reconciled with any other opinion. If he had died only for a part of the race, this language could not have been used. The phrase, 'the whole world,' is one which naturally embraces all people; is such as would be used if it be supposed that the apostle meant to teach that Christ died for all people; and is such as cannot be explained on any other supposition. If he died only for the elect, it is not true that he is the 'propitiation for the sins of the whole world' in any proper sense, nor would it be possible then to assign a sense in which it could be true. This passage, interpreted in its plain and obvious meaning, teaches the following things:

(1) that the atonement in its own nature is adapted to all people, or that it is as much fitted to one individual, or one class, as another;

(2) that it is sufficient in merit for all; that is, that if anymore should be saved than actually will be, there would be no need of any additional suffering in order to save them;

(3) that it has no special adaptedness to one person or class more than another; that is, that in its own nature it did not render the salvation of one easier than that of another. It so magnified the law, so honored God, so fully expressed the divine sense of the evil of sin in respect to all people, that the offer of salvation might be made as freely to one as to another, and that any and all might take shelter under it and be safe. Whether, however, God might not, for wise reasons, resolve that its benefits should be applied to a part only, is another question, and one which does not affect the inquiry about the intrinsic nature of the atonement. On the evidence that the atonement was made for all, see the notes at 2 Corinthians 5:14, and Hebrews 2:9.

- **Bible Knowledge Commentary:**

> *If God extends mercies to a sinning believer - and the believer does not reap the full consequences of his failure in his personal experience - that fact is not due to the merits of that believer himself. On the contrary, the grace obtained through the advocacy of Christ is to be traced, like all of God's grace, to His all-sufficient sacrifice on the cross. Should any sinning believer wonder on what grounds he might secure God's mercy after he has failed, the answer is found in this verse. So adequate is Jesus Christ as God's atoning Sacrifice that the efficacy of His work extends not merely to the sins of Christians themselves, but also to the sins of the whole world. In saying this, John was clearly affirming the view that Christ genuinely died for everyone (cf. 2 Corinthians 5:14-15,19; Hebrews 2:9). This does not mean, of course, that everyone will be saved. It means rather that anyone who hears the gospel can be saved if he so desires (Revelations 22:17).*

- **Biblical Illustrator:**

> *2. But it is asserted that He is the propitiation for 'our' sins, and not for ours only, but also for the sins of the whole world.*
>
> *(1) In the fullest, freest, and most admirable manner He has removed every barrier between us and God, and expiated of all our sins.*
>
> *(2) His love, His Cross, His religion, is not for one age, but for all ages, not for one nation or country, but for the whole world, and the promises of God give us assurance beforehand of its final triumph.*

- **Geneva Notes:**

  For men of all sorts, of all ages, and all places, so that this benefit being not to the Jews only, of whom he speaks as appears in 1 John 2:7 but also to other nations.

- **IVP Bible Background Commentary:**

  In Judaism, the sacrifice on the Day of Atonement was for Israel alone; but Jesus' sacrifice was offered not only for Christians but even for those who chose to remain God's enemies, leaving them without excuse.

- **Life Application Commentary:**

  In the phrase 'not for ours only but also for the sins of the whole world' John was reminding all believers that Christ's atoning sacrifice is sufficient for the sins of every person in the world. Martin Luther brought this point home when he explained, 'You, too, are part of the world, so that your heart cannot deceive itself and think, 'The Lord died for Peter and Paul, but not for me.' While Christ's death is sufficient for every sin of every person who ever lived or ever will live, it becomes effectual only for those who confess their sin, accept the sacrifice, and embrace Christ as Lord and Savior. John was not teaching universal salvation – that everyone was saved by Christ whether he or she believed or not. We know this from John's statements in 2:19-23; obviously the antichrists had not found forgiveness and acceptance in Christ.

- **Matthew Henry:**

  > *He is the propitiation for our sins; and not for ours only (not only for the sins of us Jews, us that are Abraham's seed according to the flesh), but also for those of the whole world (v. 2); not only for the past, or us present believers, but for the sins of all who shall hereafter believe on him or come to God through him. The extent and intent of the Mediator's death reach to all tribes, nations, and countries. As he is the only, so he is the universal atonement and propitiation for all that are saved and brought home to God, and to his favor and forgiveness.*

John 1:29 The next day John saw Jesus coming toward him and said, 'Look! The Lamb of God who takes away the sin of the world! (NLT)

- **Barnes:**

  > *Of all mankind, Jew and Gentile. His work was not to be confined to the Jew, but was also to benefit the Gentile; it was not confined to any one part of the world, but was designed to open the way of pardon to all men. He was the propitiation for the sins of the whole world, 1 John 2:2.*

- **Biblical Illustrator:**

  > *As He commands the gospel to be preached to every creature, there must be a gospel for every creature; and those who do not actually obtain salvation fail only 'because of unbelief.'*

- **Matthew Henry:**

  He takes away the sin of the world; purchases pardon for all those that repent, and believe the gospel, of what country, nation, or language, soever they be.

John 3:17 God sent his Son into the world not to judge the world, but to save the world through him. (NLT)

- **Adam Clarke:**

  God, by giving his Son, and publishing his design in giving him, shows that he purposes the salvation, not the destruction, of the world-the Gentile people: nevertheless, those who will not receive the salvation he had provided for them, whether Jews or Gentiles, must necessarily perish; for this plain reason, There is but one remedy, and they refuse to apply it.

- **Bible Knowledge Commentary:**

  God does not delight in the death of the wicked (Ezekiel 18:23,32). He desires that everyone be saved (1 Timothy2:4; 2 Peter 3:9).

- **Biblical Illustrator:**

  WHAT IS IT THAT GOD IS NOW DOING FOR US AS FALLEN SINNERS?

  1. He is giving to one sinner after another repentance and forgiveness of sins and a character unto holiness commenced and progressive. During the whole of the dispensation this is the revealed work of the Holy Spirit.

2. To separate the elect from the mass of mankind as His purchased and sanctified ones.

3. He is giving the faith which secures all this, even freedom from condemnation and acceptance in the beloved.

4. Without this faith the old condemnation remains, and a fresh condemnation is added, that following on the rejection of salvation by the only begotten Son of God.

- **Jewish New Testament:**

  In the Day of Judgment he will be the Judge who condemns the world (5:27).

- **Life Application Commentary:**

  He who believes in him is saved from God's judgment. And God wants people to believe: He is patient, 'not willing that any should perish but that all should come to repentance' (2 Peter 3:9 NKJV).

- **Wilmington Bible Handbook:**

  All are born sinners and are condemned until they accept Jesus, the cure for sin (3:18).

1 Corinthians 15:22 For as in Adam all die, even so in Christ shall all be made alive. (NLT)

- **Barnes Notes:**
  1. This act made it certain that all that came into the world would be mortal. The sentence which went forth against him (Genesis 3:19) went forth against all; affected all; involved all in the certainty of death;

2. If this passage means, that in Adam, or by him, all people became sinners, then the Corinthian's declaration 'all shall be made alive' must mean that all people shall become righteous, or that all shall be saved. (see #4, a, b, c – rs)
3. It is not a sufficient answer to this to say, that the word 'all,' in the latter part of the sentence, means all the elect, or all the righteous; for its most natural and obvious meaning is, that it is co-extensive with the word 'all' in the former part of the verse.
4. It is true LITERALLY that ALL the dead will rise: it is not true literally that all who became mortal, or became sinners by means of Adam, will be saved.
   a. The 'all' in the last clause, therefore, must be taken in a restricted sense, embracing the righteous only.
   b. The verse is to be explained on the principle of representation. Adam and Christ are the heads of their respective covenants.
   c. All represented by the one die in him, and all represented by the other live in him.
5. In Adam all die, Romans 5:12; but in Christ only those can live and rise who are justified through him, and this none are without faith in him.

- **Bible Knowledge Commentary:**

1. As the father of mankind Adam in his sin brought death to everybody (cf. Genesis 3:17-19; Roman 5:12). But because of the obedience (Philippians 2:8) of another Man (1 Timothy2:5) resurrection will come to all those related to Him by spiritual birth.

- **Biblical Illustrator:**
  1. As we have seen, even before we believe in Christ we have a better and a worse self-contending in us for the mastery.
     a. Consider the very worst man you know. Is there not a double nature in him? Has not even he a better self? Does he not know that it is the better, and that it should be supreme?
     b. This is the benefit all men derive from the redemption of Christ
     c. They have 'the Christ' in them, just as the harm they inherit from Adam is that they have 'the Adam' in them.
  2. But if all men are to live in Christ as all men die in Adam, does not the parallel involve the ultimate recovery of the whole human race? No
     a. both the Adam and the Christ are in us
     b. Adam with his 'offence,' the Christ with His 'grace'
     c. Adam with his 'disobedience,' the Christ with His 'gift of righteousness.'
     d. And we have to choose between them.
     e. Yielding to the Adam, we die;
     f. But if we yield to the Christ, we shall 'never die,' but 'reign in life' through Him.
     g. If we are not obliged to yield to Adam's sin, why should we be obliged to yield to Christ's grace?

- **Life Action Commentary Series:**
  1. Adam allowed the whole human race to succumb to death.
  2. Death is inescapable; it comes to every living thing.

3. And the reign of death over creation began because of Adam's sin.
4. Paul contrasted the roles of two single agents: Adam and Christ.
    a. Adam's sin brought condemnation and death to all
    b. Christ's sinless sacrifice and resurrection brought resurrection from the dead to all who are related to Christ through accepting his sacrifice on their behalf. Those who believe in him will be given new life.
1. At conception, we receive as part of our human inheritance the gift of death
2. At conversion, we receive Christ's gift of eternal life.
3. The choice is between death and life.

- **Matthew Henry:**

1. And so:
    a. in Adam all die, in Christ shall all be made alive;
    b. through the sin of the first Adam all men became mortal, because all derived from him the same sinful nature, so through the merit and resurrection of Christ shall all who are made to partake of the Spirit, and the spiritual nature… become immortal.
2. But the meaning is not that, as all men died in Adam, so all men, without exception, shall be made alive in Christ;
    a. the scope of the apostle's argument restrains the general meaning.

- **Wiersby Expositional Outlines:**

  1. Through the first Adam's sin that death came into the world; but through the Last Adam (Christ), death has been conquered.
  2. Christ is the firstfruits; that is, He is the first of a great harvest that is yet to come.
  3. Christ is God's 'Last Adam,' and He will reverse the wrong that the first Adam brought into this world.
  4. When Christ comes, the dead in Christ will be raised

- **Robertson Word Pictures:**

  1. All who die, die in Adam, all who will be made alive will be made alive (restored to life) in Christ.

- **Works of John Owen:**

  1. And not anywhere is it used to show forth that common resurrection which all shall have at the last day. All, then, who by virtue of the resurrection of Christ shall be made alive, are all those who are partakers of the nature of Christ...

- **Barnes:**

  > *Besides it will occur to anyone on reading the passage, that the resurrection here referred to is throughout spoken of as a vast benefit, secured by the mediation of Christ. 'The design,' says the commentator, 'is to show that the work of Christ is adapted to overcome the evils of the sin of Adam in one specific matter, that is, on the point of the resurrection. His argument, therefore, requires the apostle to show only that temporal death introduced by the first man has been counteracted by the second.'*

- **Jamieson, Fausset, and Brown:**

    In Adam all - in union of nature with Adam, the representative head of mankind in their fall. In Christ shall all - in union of nature with Christ,

- **Life Application Commentary:**

    Adam's sin brought condemnation and death to all; Christ's sinless sacrifice and resurrection brought resurrection from the dead to all who are related to Christ through accepting his sacrifice on their behalf. Those who believe in him will be given new life.

- **Francis Chan:**

    In looking at these passages (Chan is discussing the word "all" – rs), one Christian Universalist says, 'Paul envisioned a time when all persons would be reconciled to God in the full redemptive sense. Is that what these passages are saying, or is there something else going on?

    There seems to be something else going on in 1 Corinthians 15:22, for instance, where Paul says, 'In Christ all will be made alive' (NIV). The verse by itself could mean that everyone will end up being saved, but the context doesn't support this interpretation. When Paul says 'all will be made alive,' he's clearly thinking about the resurrection of believers at the second coming of Christ. In fact, he says this very thing in the next verse: 'All will be made alive at his coming' (see vv.22-23). So the verse can't mean that everyone will be saved in the end. In fact, following this verse is a whole lot of destruction: destruction of everyone and everything that opposes God in this life (vv 25-26).

> ... *You've got to figure out from the context what 'all' means. For instance, when Mark said that, 'all the country of Judea' and 'all the people of Jerusalem' were going out to be baptized by John (Mark 1:5 NASB), he certainly didn't mean every single individual in Judea – man, woman, and child. 'All' here simply denotes a large number of people. In Acts 21:28, Paul is accused of preaching to 'all men everywhere' (NASB). Did Paul really share the gospel with every single person on earth?*
>
> ... *The 'all' who will be 'made alive' in Christ refers to believers of all types, not every single person.*

1 Timothy 2:3 This is good and pleases God our Savior, 4 who wants everyone to be saved and to understand the truth. 5 For there is only one God and one Mediator who can reconcile God and humanity—the man Christ Jesus. 6 He gave his life to purchase freedom for everyone. This is the message God gave to the world at just the right time. (NLT)

- **Works of John Owen:**

    1. The will of God is usually distinguished into his will intending and his will commanding; or rather, that word is used in reference unto God in this twofold notion

    2. For his purpose, what he will do;

    3. For his approbation of what we do, with his command thereof. Let now our opposers take their option in whether signification the will of God shall be here understood, or how he willeth the salvation of all.

    4. 'God commandeth all men to use the means whereby they may obtain the end, or salvation, the performance whereof is acceptable to God in any or

all;' and so it is the same with that of the apostle in another place, 'God commandeth all men everywhere to repent.' Now, if this be the way whereby God willeth the salvation of all here mentioned, then certainly those all can possibly be no more than to whom he granteth and… the means of grace; which are indeed a great many, but yet not the one hundredth part of the posterity of Adam. Besides, taking God's willing the salvation of men in this sense, we deny the sequel of the first proposition, — namely, that Christ died for as many as God thus willeth should be saved.

5. the will of God be taken for:
   a. his efficacious will,
   b. the will of his purpose and good pleasure (as truly to me it seems exceedingly evident that that is here intended)
   c. the will of God is made the ground and bottom of our supplications; as if in these our prayers we should say only, 'Thy will be done,' — which is to have them all to be saved: now, we have a promise to receive of God 'whatsoever we ask according to his will,' 1 John 3:22; 5:14;
   d. therefore this will of God, which is here proposed as the ground of our prayers, must needs be his effectual or rather efficacious will, which is always accomplished
   e. then certainly it must be fulfilled, and all those saved whom he would have saved; for whatsoever God can do and will do, that shall certainly come to pass and be effected.
   f. That God can save all (not considering his decree) none doubts; and that he will save all it is here affirmed: therefore, if these all here

be all and everyone, all and everyone shall certainly be saved. 'Let us eat and drink, for tomorrow we shall die.' 'Who hath resisted God's will?' Romans 9:19. 'He hath done whatsoever he hath pleased,' Psalms 115:3. 'He doeth according to his will in the army of heaven, and among the inhabitants of the earth,' Daniel 4:35.

g. If all, then, here be to be understood of all men universally, one of these two things must of necessity follow: — either that God faileth of his purpose and intention, or else that all men universally shall be saved; which puts us upon the second thing considerable in the words, namely, who are meant by all men in this place.

6. By all men the apostle here intendeth all sorts of men indefinitely living under the gospel, or in these latter times, under the enlarged dispensation of the means of grace.

a. That men of these times only are intended is the acknowledgment of Arminius himself, treating with Perkins about this place.

b. The scope of the apostle, treating of the amplitude, enlargement, and extent of grace, in the outward administration thereof, under the gospel, will not suffer it to be denied.

c. This he lays down as a foundation of our praying for all, — because the means of grace and the habitation of the church is now no longer confined to the narrow bounds of one nation, but promiscuously and indefinitely extended unto all people, tongues, and languages; and to all sorts of men amongst them, high and low, rich and poor, one with another.

    d. We say, then, that by the words all men are here intended only of all sorts of men, suitable to the purpose of the apostle, which was to show that all external difference between the sons of men is now taken away;

7. The word all being in the Scripture most commonly used in this sense (that is, for many of all sorts), and there being nothing in the subject-matter of which it is here affirmed that should in the least measure impel to another acceptation of the word, especially for a universal collection of every individual, we hold it safe to cleave to the most usual sense and meaning of it. Thus, our Savior is said to cure all diseases, and the Pharisees to tithe pa=n la/xanon, Luke 11:42.

8. Paul himself plainly leadeth us to this interpretation of it; for after he hath enjoined us to pray for all, because the Lord will have all to be saved, he expressly intimates that by all men he understandeth men of all sorts, ranks, conditions, and orders,

9. where all the people is interpreted to be some of all sorts, by a distribution of them into the several orders, classes, and conditions whereof they were.

10. all shall be saved whom God will have to be saved; this we dare not deny, for 'who hath resisted his will?' Seeing, then, it is most certain that all shall not be saved (for some shall stand on the left hand), it cannot be that the universality of men should be intended in this place.

11. If he would have had them all come to the knowledge of the truth, why did he show his word to some and not to others, without which they could not attain thereunto?

a. 'He suffered all nations' in former ages 'to walk in their own ways,'

b. Acts 14:16, and 'winked at the time of this ignorance,'

c. Acts 17:30, hiding the mystery of salvation from those former ages,

d. Colossians 1:26, continuing the same dispensation even until this day in respect of some; and that because 'so it seemeth good in his sight,' Matthew 11:25, 26.

e. It is, then, evident that God doth not will that all and everyone in the world, of all ages and times, should come to the knowledge of the truth, but only all sorts of men without difference; and, therefore, they only are here intended.

- **Bible Knowledge Commentary:**

    John's goal was that all men might come to trust in Jesus.

John 12:32 And when I am lifted up from the earth, I will draw everyone to myself." 33 He said this to indicate how he was going to die. (NLT)

- **Barnes Notes:**

1. I will incline all kinds of men; or will make the way open by the cross, so that all men may come. I will provide a way which shall present a strong motive or inducement-the strongest that can be presented to all men to come to me.

- **Bible Knowledge Commentary:**

  1. Jesus said that at the cross He would draw all men to Himself. He did not mean everybody will be saved for He made it clear that some will be lost (John 5:28-29).
  2. If the drawing by the Son is the same as that of the Father (6:44), it means He will draw indiscriminately. Those saved will include not only Jews, but also those from every tribe, language, people, and nation (Revelations 5:9; cf. John 10:16; 11:52).

- **Jamieson, Fausset, Brown:**

  1. And does not the death of the Cross in all its significance, revealed in the light, and borne in upon the heart by the power, of the Holy Spirit, possess an attraction over the wide world-to civilized and savage, learned and illiterate alike-which breaks down all opposition, assimilates all to itself,

- **Life Application Commentary:**

  1. That Jesus will draw all people to himself does not mean that everyone will ultimately be saved.
  2. Jesus has already made it clear that some will not be saved (5:28-29).
  3. Rather like his word whoever in verse 26, Jesus was saying that his offer of salvation extends to all people, not just to the Jews.
  4. Jesus' incredible love, expressed in his death for all people, will draw and unify those who believe, so that sin, evil, and death (the weapons of the prince of this world) will be powerless.

John 5:25 "And I assure you that the time is coming, indeed it's here now, when the dead will hear my voice—the

voice of the Son of God. And those who listen will live. 26 The Father has life in himself, and he has granted that same life-giving power to his Son. 27 And he has given him authority to judge everyone because he is the Son of Man. 28 Don't be so surprised! Indeed, the time is coming when all the dead in their graves will hear the voice of God's Son, 29 and they will rise again. Those who have done good will rise to experience eternal life, and those who have continued in evil will rise to experience judgment. (NLT)

- **Adam Clarke:**

> *Three kinds of death are mentioned in the Scriptures: natural, spiritual, and eternal.*
>
> *The first consists in the separation of the body and soul.*
>
> *The second in the separation of God and the soul.*
>
> *The third in the separation of body and soul from God in the other world.*
>
> *Answerable to these three kinds of death, there is a threefold life: Natural life, which consists in the union of the soul and body. Spiritual life, which consists in the union of God and the soul, by faith and love. Eternal life, which consists in the communion of the body and soul with God, by holiness, in the realms of bliss.*

- **Barnes Notes:**

> *To do judgment-that is, to judge. He has appointment to 'do justice;' to see that the universe suffers no wrong, either by the escape of the guilty or by the punishment of the innocent.*
>
> *The doctrine of those Universalists who hold that all people will be saved immediately at death, therefore, cannot*

be true. This passage provides that at the day of judgment the wicked will be condemned. Let it be added that if 'then' condemned they will be lost forever. Thus, in Matthew 25:46, it is said to be 'everlasting' punishment; 2 Thessalonians 1:8-9, it is called 'everlasting' destruction. There is no account of redemption in hell-no Savior, no Holy Spirit, no offer of mercy there.

- **Biblical Illustrator:**

   Those who would not hear the voice of mercy must hear that of judgment.

- **Jamieson, Fausset, and Brown Commentary:**

   It would have been harsh, as Bengel remarks, to say, 'the resurrection of death,' though that is meant; because sinners rise only from death to death. The resurrection of both classes is an exercise of sovereign authority; but in the one case it is an act of grace, in the other of justice. Compare Daniel 12:2, from which the language is taken. How awfully grand are these unfoldings of His dignity and authority from the mouth of Christ Himself! And they are all, it will be observed, uttered in the third person- as great principles and arrangements from everlasting, independent of the utterance of them on this occasion. Immediately after this, however, He resumes the first person.

- **Life Application Commentary:**

   Every person will be resurrected when the Lord returns, with one of two results: one will be life, the other will be condemnation. God grants eternal life to those who have come to the Light and have believed in Jesus Christ. But God will judge and condemn those who rebelled against Christ by refusing to come to the Light. God's judgment has already come upon them and will be completely executed by the Son of Man after the resurrection (see 3:18-21).

- **Barnes:**

The word 'damnation' means the sentence passed on one by a judge-judgment or condemnation. The word, as we use it, applies only to the judgment pronounced by God on the wicked; but this is not its meaning always in the Bible. Here it has, however, that meaning. Those who have done evil will be raised up 'to be condemned or damned.' This will be the object in raising them up-this the sole design. It is elsewhere said that they shall then be condemned to everlasting punishment (Matthew 25:46), and that they shall be punished with everlasting destruction (2 Thessalonians 1:8-9); and it is said of the unjust that they are reserved unto the day of judgment to be punished, 2 Peter 2:9. That this refers to the future judgment-to the resurrection then, and not to anything that takes place in this life-is clear from the following considerations:

1. Jesus had just spoken of what would be done in this life-of the power of the gospel, John 5:25. He adds here that something still more wonderful-something BEYOND this-would take place. 'All that are in the graves' shall hear his voice.

2. He speaks of those who are in their graves, evidently referring to the dead. Sinners are sometimes said to be dead in sin, but sinners are not said to be 'in a grave.' This is applied in the Scriptures only to those who are deceased.

3. The language used here of the 'righteous' cannot be applied to anything in this life. When God converts men, it is not because they 'have been good.'

4. Nor is the language employed of the evil applicable to anything here. In what condition among men can it be said, with any appearance of sense that they are brought forth from their graves to the resurrection of damnation? The doctrine of those Universalists who hold that all people will be saved immediately at death, therefore, cannot be true. This passage proves that at the day of judgment the wicked will be condemned. Let it be added that if 'then' condemned they will be lost forever. Thus, in Matthew 25:46, it is said to be 'everlasting' punishment; 2 Thessalonians 1:8-9, it is called 'everlasting' destruction. There is no account of redemption in hell-no Savior, no Holy Spirit, no offer of mercy there.

John 6:44 For no one can come to me unless the Father who sent me draws them to me, and at the last day I will raise them up. (NLT)

- **Bible Knowledge Commentary:**

No one can come to Jesus or believe on Him without divine help. People are so ensnared in the quicksand of sin and unbelief that unless God draws them (cf. v. 65), they are hopeless. This drawing of God is not limited to a few. Jesus said, 'I... will draw all men to, Myself' (12:32). This does not mean that all will be saved but that Greeks (i.e., Gentiles; 12:20) as well as Jews will be saved. Those who will be saved will also be resurrected (cf. 6:39-40).

Matthew 25:46 "And they will go away into eternal punishment, but the righteous will go into eternal life." (NLT)

- **Adam Clarke:**

> No appeal, no remedy, to all eternity! No end to the punishment of those whose final impenitence manifests in them an eternal will and desire to sin. By dying in a settled opposition to God, they cast themselves into a necessity of continuing in an eternal aversion from him.
>
> But some are of opinion that this punishment shall have an end: this is as likely as that the glory of the righteous shall have an end: for the same word is used to express the duration of the punishment, kolasin aioonion, as is used to express the duration of the state of glory: zooeen aioonion. I have seen the best things that have been written in favor of the final redemption of damned spirits; but I never saw an answer to the argument against that doctrine, drawn from this verse, but what sound learning and criticism should be ashamed to acknowledge. The original word aioon is certainly to be taken here in its proper grammatical sense, continued being, aieioon, NEVER ENDING. Some have gone a middle way, and think that the wicked shall be annihilated. This, I think, is contrary to the text; if they go into punishment, they continue to exist; for that which ceases to be, ceases to suffer. See the note at Genesis 21:33, where the whole subject is explained.
>
> From what our Lord has here said, we may see that God indispensably requires of every man to bring forth good fruit; and that a fruitless tree shall be inevitably cut down, and cast into the fire. Let it be also remarked that

God does not here impute to his own children the good works which Jesus Christ did for them.

- **Barnes:**

These 'persons.' Many, holding the doctrine of universal salvation have contended that God would punish sin only. Christ says that 'those on his left hand,' shall go away-not 'sins,' but 'sinners.' Besides, sin, as an abstract thing, cannot be punished. Sin is nothing but an 'act' - the act of a transgressor, and, to be reached at all, it must be reached by punishing the offender himself.

The original word translated here as 'punishment' means torment, or suffering inflicted for crime. The noun is used but in one other place in the New Testament - 1 John 4:18: 'Fear hath 'torment.' The verb from which the noun is derived is twice used - Acts 4:21; 2 Peter 2:9. In all these places it denotes anguish, suffering, punishment. It does not mean simply a 'state or condition,' but absolute, positive suffering; and if this word does not teach it, no word 'could' express the idea that the wicked would suffer. It has been contended that the sufferings of the wicked will not be ETERNAL or WITHOUT END. It is not the purpose of these notes to enter into debates of that kind further than to ascertain the meaning of the language used by the sacred writers. In regard to the meaning of the word 'everlasting' in this place, it is to be observed:

that the LITERAL *meaning of the word expresses absolute eternity – 'always belong,' Matthew 18:8; 19:16; Mark 3:29; Romans 2:7; Hebrews 5:9.*

Admitting that it was the Savior's design ALWAYS *to teach this doctrine, this would be 'the very word' to express it; and if this does not teach it, it could* NOT *be taught.*

That it is not taught in any plainer manner in any confession of faith on the globe; and if this may be explained away, all those may be.

That our Savior knew that this would be so understood by nine-tenths of the world; and if he did not mean to teach it, he has knowingly led them into error, and his honesty cannot be vindicated.

That he knew that the doctrine was calculated to produce 'fear and terror;' and if he was benevolent, and actually used language calculated to produce this fear and terror, his conduct cannot be vindicated in exciting unnecessary alarms.

That the word used here is the same in the original as that used to express the eternal life of the righteous; if one can be proved to be limited in duration, the other can by the same arguments.

- **Bible Exposition Commentary:**

This kingdom was prepared for these saved individuals, but Matthew 25:41 does not state that the everlasting fire was prepared for the goats. It was prepared for the devil and his angels (Revelations 20:10). God never prepared hell for people. There is no evidence from Scripture that God predestines people to go to hell. If sinners listen to Satan, and follow his ways, they will end up where he ends up - in the torments of hell. There are only two eternal destinies: everlasting punishment for those who reject Christ or eternal life for those who trust Him.

- **Biblical Illustrator:**

> Your opinion about 'forever' can have no manner of effect upon the reality of that 'forever.'... You have a strong opinion that hell-fire is a delusion; that they are superstitious, and cruel, and ignorant who ask you to pause, and awake, and prepare for this coming, this continued retribution; but your opinions will not have the slightest, the remotest, the minutest influence on the tremendous fact.

Romans 4:16 So the promise is received by faith. It is given as a free gift. And we are all certain to receive it, whether or not we live according to the law of Moses, if we have faith like Abraham's. For Abraham is the father of all who believe. (NLT)

- **Biblical Illustrator:**

> THE END IN VIEW – that 'the promise may be sure to all the seed.' Every promise of God is sure in the sense of being trustworthy. But the fulfilment is not necessarily sure to any, for they come short of its stipulations. The certainty here is the opposite of what is deprecated in ver. 4: 'the promise being made of none effect,' i.e., falling short of its full accomplishment.

It is 'of faith.' Why? Simply, that it may still be all 'by grace.' We have seen that it is by grace alone that any are admitted into fellowship with the Son in His gracious work and ministry of substitution. Let us now see what grace there is in the terms, or the manner, of their admission, freely, unreservedly, unconditionally; if they will; when they will. Ah! But does not this really destroy all certainty? If they will! Does it not cast doubt on everything? When they will! When will they? Will they ever? Of what avail then is all this grace to them? And yet how can the thing be otherwise? How can any enter into union with the Son, so as to have the promise made sure to them in Him, otherwise than by its being freely left to their own free choice? If the grace is to be free, it must be not only freely given, but freely taken. There can be no coercion. There must be cordial and congenial consent. No otherwise can the promise be sure to beings capable of choice. Their free, unforced yes must be got. And if that yes be got, all is safe. Hence the necessity of faith,

- **Geneva Notes:**

The conclusion of this argument: the salvation and justification of the posterity of Abraham (that is, of the Church which is composed of all believers) proceeds from faith which lays hold on the promise made to Abraham, and which promise Abraham himself first of all laid hold on.

- **Life Application Commentary:**

> Abraham is the father of all who come to God in faith, whether they are Jews or Gentiles.
>
> Paul explains that Abraham had pleased God through faith alone, before Abraham had ever heard about the rituals that would become so important to the Jewish people. We too are saved by faith plus nothing. It is not by loving God and doing good that we are saved; neither is it by faith plus love or by faith plus good deeds. We are saved only through faith in Christ, trusting him to forgive all our sins.

Hebrews 10:38 And my righteous ones will live by faith. But I will take no pleasure in anyone who turns away.' 39 But we are not like those who turn away from God to their own destruction. We are the faithful ones, whose souls will be saved. (NLT)

- **Adam Clarke:**

> As dastards and cowards are hated by all men, so those that slink away from Christ and his cause, for fear of persecution or secular loss, God must despise; in them he cannot delight; and his spirit, grieved with their conduct, must desert their hearts, and lead them to darkness and hardness.

- **Barnes:**

> He will be a man exposed to the divine wrath; a man on whom God cannot look but with

disapprobation. By this solemn consideration, therefore, the apostle urges on them the importance of perseverance, and the guilt and danger of apostasy from the Christian faith. If such a case should occur, no matter what might have been the former condition, and no matter what love or zeal might have been evinced, yet such an apostasy would expose the individual to the certain wrath of God. His former love could not save him, any more than the former obedience of the angels saved them from the horrors of eternal chains and darkness, or than the holiness in which Adam was created saved him and his posterity from the calamities which his apostasy incurred.

- **The Biblical Illustrator:**

Some who once were accounted disciples of Christ have drawn back into open profanity and infidelity (2 Peter 2:20, 21). Persons of this character, who have stifled conviction, and hold the truth in unrighteousness, become generally the most hardened and daring in wickedness. Common restraints are removed – the voice of conscience is silenced – the Spirit of God ceases to strive, and they are given over to a reprobate mind – to fill up the measure of their iniquities, and at last to perish in unbelief.

Daniel 12:2 Many of those whose bodies lie dead and buried will rise up, some to everlasting life and some to shame and everlasting disgrace. (NLT)

- **Barnes:**

> Not a few interpreters, therefore, have understood this in the sense of all, considered as referring to a multitude, or as suggesting the idea of a multitude, or keeping up the idea that there would be great numbers. If this is the proper interpretation, the word 'many' was used instead of the word 'all' to suggest to the mind the idea that there would be a multitude, or that there would be a great number.
>
> Another portion in such a way that they shall have only shame or dishonor. The Hebrew word means reproach, contumely; and it may be applied to the reproach which one casts on another, Job 16:10; Ps 39:8 (9); 79:12; or to the reproach which rests on anyone, Joshua 5:9; Isa 54:4. Here the word means the reproach or dishonor which would rest on them for their sins, their misconduct, and their evil deeds.
>
> If it be interpreted as applying to the resurrection of the dead, it means that the wicked would rise to reproach and shame before the universe for their folly and vileness. As a matter of fact, one of the bitterest ingredients in the doom of the wicked will be the shame and confusion with which they will be overwhelmed in the great day on account of the sins and follies of their course in this world.
>
> The word translated 'everlasting' (punishment) is the same which is rendered 'eternal' (life), and means what is to endure forever. So the Greek here, where the same word occurs, as in Matthew 25:46 – 'some to everlasting

life,' eis zooeen aioonion, 'and some to everlasting contempt.' aischuneen aioonion - is one which would denote a strict and proper eternity. The word 'contempt' draa°own means, properly, a repulse; and then aversion, abhorrence. The meaning here is aversion or abhorrence-the feeling with which we turn away from what is loathsome, disgusting, or hateful.

- **Biblical Illustrator:**

    The righteous will be raised to life eternal; the wicked to 'damnation.' The point in the lesson we would enforce – and it is a tremendous point in the matter of personal interest – is embraced in one word 'which?' One or the other of these experiences life before each and every child of Adam. Do what we will, and neglect what we will, we shall have a part in this resurrection; we shall 'hear the voice of the Son of God' then, whether we hear it now or not; and we 'shall live,' and 'come forth' either to be caught up into Heaven, or be banished to hell! In that hour of infinite power and display there will be no place of retreat, no possible concealment of evasion.

Rom 3:24 Yet God, with undeserved kindness, declares that we are righteous. He did this through Christ Jesus when he freed us from the penalty for our sins. 25 For God presented Jesus as the sacrifice for sin. People are made right with God when they believe that Jesus sacrificed his life, shedding his blood. This sacrifice shows that God was being fair when he held back and did not punish those who sinned in times past, 26 for he was looking ahead and

including them in what he would do in this present time. God did this to demonstrate his righteousness, for he himself is fair and just, and he declares sinners to be right in his sight when they believe in Jesus.

27 Can we boast, then, that we have done anything to be accepted by God? No, because our acquittal is not based on obeying the law. It is based on faith. 28 So we are made right with God through faith and not by obeying the law.

29 After all, is God the God of the Jews only? Isn't he also the God of the Gentiles? Of course he is. 30 There is only one God, and he makes people right with himself only by faith, whether they are Jews or Gentiles. (NLT)

1. People are made right with God when **they** believe not 'of faith' of Jesus
2. OT and NT / Church Age are saved by the same manner
3. God declares sinners right when **they** believe in Jesus (the penalty has been paid for since the cross but it is not the possession of the individual until they believe)
4. So we are made right with God **through** our faith and only **by our** faith

Ephesians 2:8 God saved you by his grace when you believed. And you can't take credit for this; it is a gift from God. (NLT)

- **Adam Clarke:**

> By this grace ye are saved through faith; and THIS (touto, this salvation) is not of you; it is the gift of God, not of works: so that no one can boast. 'The relative touto, this, which is in the neuter gender, cannot stand for pistis, faith, which

is the feminine; but it has the whole sentence that goes before for its antecedent.'

Without the grace or power to believe no man ever did or can believe; but with that power the act of faith is a man's own.

God never believes for any man, no more than he repents for him; the penitent, through this grace enabling him, believes for himself: nor does he believe necessarily, or impulsively when he has that power; the power to believe may be present long before it is exercised, else, why the solemn warnings with which we meet everywhere in the word of God, and threatenings against those who do not believe? Is not this a proof that such persons have the power but do not use it? They believe not, and therefore are not established.

- **Barnes:**

It is not God that 'believes' for him, for that is impossible.

But the Holy Spirit does not 'repent' for us. It is our 'own mind' that repents; our own heart that feels; our own eyes that weep—and without this there can be no true repentance. No one can repent for another; and God neither can nor ought to repent; for us. He has done no wrong, and if repentance is ever exercised, therefore, it must be exercised by our own minds.

So of faith. God cannot believe for us. 'We' must believe, or 'we' shall be damned.

Galatians 1:8 Let God's curse fall on anyone, including us or even an angel from heaven, who preaches a different kind of Good News than the one we preached to you. (NLT)

- **Adam Clarke:**

  Were I to preach any other, I should incur the curse of God.

  Leave them to that God who will show his displeasure against all who corrupt, all who add to, and all who take from the word of his revelation.

- **Bible Knowledge Commentary:**

  If he (a divinely called apostle) or an angel (a heavenly messenger) were to alter the gospel message - a highly improbable situation - then let him be accursed or eternally condemned (anathema).

- **Biblical Illustrator:**

  A Universalist preached to a chance audience, and, at its close, offered to preach again at a future day; when an old Friend arose, and said, 'If thou hast told the truth this time, we do not need thee anymore; and, if thou hast told us a lie, we do not want thee anymore.'

1 Corinthians 11:32 Yet when we are judged by the Lord, we are being disciplined so that we will not be condemned along with the world. (NLT)

- **Barnes:**

> The sense is, that though they were thus afflicted by God; though he had manifested his displeasure at the manner in which they had observed the ordinance, yet the divine judgment in the case was not inexorable.
>
> [That we should not be condemned with the world] It is implied here:
>
> That the world-those who were not Christians, would be condemned;

- **Life Application Commentary:**

> The world will face eternal condemnation because it has rejected Christ.

Matthew 7:13 "You can enter God's Kingdom only through the narrow gate. The highway to hell is broad, and its gate is wide for the many who choose that way. 14 But the gateway to life is very narrow and the road is difficult, and only a few ever find it. (NLT)

- **Adam Clarke:**

> With those who say it means repentance, and forsaking sin, I can have no controversy. That is certainly a gate, and a strait one too, through which every sinner must turn to God, in order to find salvation.
>
> And very broad, euruchooros, from eurus, broad, and choora, a place, a spacious roomy place, that leadeth forward, apagousa, into THAT

destruction, eis teen apooleian, meaning eternal misery;

So, says Christ, is the path to heaven. It is narrow. It is not 'the great highway' that people tread. Few go there. Here and there one may be seen-traveling in solitude and singularity. The way to death, on the other hand, is broad. Multitudes are in it. It is the great highway in which people go. They fall into it easily and without effort, and go without thought. If they wish to leave that and go by a narrow gate to the city, it would require effort and thought. So, says Christ, 'diligence' is needed to enter life.

- **The Bible Exposition Commentary:**

  These are, of course, the way to heaven and the way to hell. The broad way is the easy way; it is the popular way. But we must not judge spiritual profession by statistics; the majority is not always right.

- **Matthew Henry:**

  There are but two ways, right and wrong, good and evil; the way to heaven, and the way to hell; in the one of which we are all of us walking:

  Death, eternal death, is at the end of it (and the way of sin tends to it), —everlasting destruction from the presence of the Lord.

  Those that are going to heaven are but few, compared to those that are going to hell; a remnant, a little flock, like the grape-gleanings of the vintage; as the eight that were saved in the ark, 1 Peter 3:20.

- **Wilmington Bible Handbook:**

  The highway to destruction is wide and well-traveled. The gateway to life is narrow and little used. More people will miss eternal life than find it.

Gal 2:20 I am crucified with Christ: nevertheless I live; yet not I, but Christ liveth in me: and the life which I now live in the flesh I live by the faith of the Son of God, who loved me, and gave himself for me. (KJV)

- **Barnes:**

  By confidence in the Son of God, looking to him for strength, and trusting in his promises, and in his grace.

- **Bible Knowledge Commentary:**

  Yet Christ does not operate automatically in a believer's life; it is a matter of living the new life by faith in the Son of God. It is then faith and not works or legal obedience that releases divine power to live a Christian life. This faith, stated Paul, builds on the sacrifice of Christ who loved us and gave Himself for us.

- **Biblical Illustrator:**

And now you will see what part faith plays in the matter. Obviously it is the connecting link betwixt that Incarnate Truth and my inner self. Here is a man who once did not see, and therefore could not believe it. And he had no Divine life in him – nothing but what was perishable; all of it, its joys, hopes, attainments – perishable. But, he came at last to see, aye, to believe. The reading, the saying, the preaching, was fact in his esteem. And immediately – as the fluid flies along the galvanic wire when it has contact – immediately, by the contact of a living faith, a faith of the heart, the influence, the vitalizing, Divine force of that truth begins to flood his being, and he begins to live a life that shall never rile.

The apostle had said before, that 'we are justified by faith alone, and not by the works of the law;' and that a believer was crucified with Christ. Now, says he, this doctrine that I have preached unto you, is no way opposite unto our spiritual life, or unto our holiness; yet, now I live, or 'nevertheless I live.'

I. EVERY TRUE BELIEVER, EVERY GODLY, GRACIOUS MAN, IS A LIVING MAN, lives a spiritual life, is in the state of life (John 6:40,47,48,54,55).

1. What is this spiritual life?

(1) It is a supernatural perfection (Ephesians 4:18).

(2) It rises from our union with Christ by the Spirit.

(3) It is that supernatural perfection whereby a man is able to act, and move, and work towards God as his utmost and last end.

2. Whereby may it appear, that every godly, gracious man, is thus a living man, made partaker of this spiritual life, so as to be able to act, and move, and work towards God as his utmost end?

The faith of the Son of God: – So called because –

I. He is the REVELATIONSEALER of it (John 1:17).

II. He is the AUTHOR of it (Hebrews 12:2).

III. He is the OBJECT of it.

WHAT IS THIS FAITH? Faith is a grace, by which we believe God's Word in general, and in a special manner do receive Christ, and rest upon Him for grace here and glory hereafter.

1. There is assent.

2. Consent.

3. Affiance. Resting on Christ.

II. HOW, AND WHY, ARE WE SAID TO LIVE BY FAITH? Distinct graces have their distinct offices. In Scripture language we are said to live by faith, but to work by love.

There must be life before operation. Now we are said to live by faith –

1. Because it is the grace that unites us to Christ.

2. Because all other graces are marshalled and ranked under the conduct of faith. It is the first stone in the spiritual building, to which all the rest are added. Without faith, virtue would languish, our command over our passions be weak, and the

back of patience quite broken, and our care of the-knowledge of Divine things very small.

3. Because whatever is ascribed to faith, redounds to the honor of Christ. The worth lies in the object, as the ivy receives strength from the oak round which it winds. Faith does all, not from any intrinsic worth and force in itself; but all its power is in dependence upon Christ. We are said to live by faith, as we are said to be fed by the hand; it is the instrument.

4. Because faith removes obstructions, and opens the passages of grace, that it may run more freely. Expectation is the opening of the soul (Psalm 81:10).

The faith which is the life of the soul, is not mere belief of the existence of God, and of those great moral and religious truths which are the foundation of all religion. Nor does the faith of Christ, spoken of here, mean faith in that unseen world which Christ has revealed. Nor is the truth in question either exhausted or accurately stated by saying, the faith which has this life-giving power has the whole Word of God for its object. It is, indeed, admitted that faith has respect to the whole revelation of God. It receives all His doctrines, bows to all His commands, trembles at His threatenings, and rejoices at His promises. This, however, is not the faith by which the apostle lived; or, rather, it is not those acts of faith which have the truth of God in general for their object, which gives life to the soul. The doctrine of the text and of the whole New Testament is, that the soul is saved, that spiritual life is obtained, by those acts of faith which have Christ for their object. Other things in the Word of God we may not know, and, therefore, may not consciously believe, but Christ we must know. About other things true Christians may differ, but they must all agree as to what they believe concerning Christ. He is, in such a sense, the object of faith, that saving faith consists in receiving and resting on Him alone for salvation, as He is offered to us in the gospel, it consists in receiving Christ, i.e., in recognizing, acknowledging, accepting, and appropriating Him, as He is held forth to us in the Scripture. It includes, therefore, a resting on Him alone for salvation, i.e., for justification, sanctification, and eternal life (Romans 3:21-31; Philippians 3:1-14; 1 John 5:1, etc.).

- **Jamieson, Fausset, and Brown:**

    Greek, 'IN faith (namely), that of, (i.e., which rests on) the, Son of God.' 'In faith' answers by contrast to 'in the flesh.' Faith, not the flesh, is the real element in which I live. The phrase, 'the Son of God,' reminds us that His divine Sonship is the source of His life-giving power (John 5:26). S

- **Jewish New Testament Commentary:**

    Because the Messiah lives in me, I am able to live by the same trusting faithfulness that the Son of God had (see v. 16cN), which enabled him to love me and give himself up for me. My entire life must be imbued by this spirit; anything else, anything less falls short of faith in and faithfulness to Yeshua the Messiah.

It is my prayer that, the sages from the past being dead... still speak (Hebrews 11:4). I have endeavored to be "fair" in sharing the experts. If they said the verse would lend towards Universalism, I included the quote. However, I feel it is equally "fair" to admit that the majority of the writers stood in an opposite position than Christian Hopeful Universalism.

Look at the information given... spend time in prayer with God... listen to the Holy Spirit in your gut... And declare your faith.

Textual Considerations For the word "All"

My favorite movie is "Fiddler on the Roof." There is a particular scene in the beginning that succinctly describes the problem with language. Allow me to set the scene for you. Tevia, the main character, is in the town square giving his milk and cheese to the citizens. A group gathers and discusses the current events in the world. An opinion is shared with the group by an elder citizen. Tevia replies, "You are right." A young man standing by gives a completely opposite view and Tevia replies, "You are right." One of the observers looks at Tevia and asks, "He is right, and he is right (pointing to the two opinion givers)? They both can't be right." To which Tevia replies, "You are also right."

It is difficult for a parent to communicate in the same language with their teenager. Or how often have two people been in a conversation, using the same language, only to realize they are talking about different things?

Back to the Fiddler. The town's butcher, a widower, is interested in speaking with Tevia to arrange a marriage between the butcher and Tevia's oldest daughter. The town matchmaker instructs Tevia to speak with the butcher, but Tevia has no idea why. A visit is made to the butcher's home and the two men begin talking. The butcher speaks about his loneliness and need for companionship which leads to asking for the daughter's hand. Tevia misinterprets his friend and thinks the butcher wants to purchase Tevia's new milk cow, and can't understand why or how his cow will help with the loneliness. The conversation quickly deteriorates as one is thinking of an arranged marriage while the other is assuming the cow is the subject. Soon, laughter breaks out as they clarify what their meaning to say in the conversation.

That's life. It happens often - saying one thing while the other person misinterprets your words or purpose. It is no different with the Bible. There are two primary languages used in the original writing of the Bible. The Old Testament was primarily in Hebrew, while the New Testament was written in Greek.

Few of us have a clear and effective understanding of these languages, and those who are skilled in their use are students who have learned from the sages of the past. So, when dealing with the Bible and endeavoring to establish a view on doctrinal truth, we must rely on the masters. But even then, the masters disagree on many points. Therefore, it is wise to establish the boundary of accepting as truth those precepts that the majority of masters are in agreement with rather than those "lone wolf" interpretations. This allows acceptance of a belief while knowing it is not in disagreement with the majority.

This is a common practice in our daily life. If your doctor tells you that you have a disease and should begin a specific course of treatment, one would be wise to secure a second or possibly even a third opinion. And, you would want those opinions to be from professionals with as much, if not more, education and experience as your current specialist. Furthermore, you would likely select the course prescribed by the majority of the preeminent experts.

Following are my notes from my textual study surrounding the word "all." My desire is to understand what God meant when He said, "all in Adam die," and "all are made alive in Christ". Is He speaking of universalism or not?

I also want to help the reader establish sound beliefs regarding the doctrine of salvation.

Textual consideration of the word "all":

- **Textual Commentary Greek New Testament:**
  1. The reading pa/nta, which suggests ideas of a cosmic redemption may have arisen under the influence of Colossians 1:16-17 and/or Gnostic speculation.

- **Wiersbe Expository Outlines:**
  1. This does not mean all people without exception, but all people regardless of race.

- **Robertson Word Pictures:**
  1. By 'all men' pantas Jesus does not mean every individual man, for some, as Simeon said (Luke 2:34) are repelled by Christ, but this is the way that Greeks (John 12:22) can and will come to Christ, by the way of the Cross, the only way to the Father (John 14:6).

- **The USB New Testament Handbook:**
  1. However, in some manuscripts the Greek neuter plural (panta) appears. This neuter form in Greek is ambiguous and may have the meaning of 'everyone,' 'all things,' or 'all.'
  2. The stronger manuscript evidence is in support of the masculine plural ('all men').
  3. The idea of a cosmic redemption, suggested by the neuter plural, represents more closely the theology of such a passage as Colossians 1:16-17.
  4. The UBS Committee on the Greek text decided in favor of the reading 'all men,' evaluating their decision as a 'D' choice, which indicates a very high degree of doubt concerning the reading selected.

- **Thayers Greek Lexicon:**

NT: 3956 pas, pasa, pan = all, every

Adjectivally with anarthrous nouns (without the definite article)

a. any, every one

b. any and every, of every kind Matthew 4:23

c. the whole Matthew 2:3

With nouns which have the article, all the, the whole Matthew 8:32

Without a substantive:

Masculine and feminine every one, any one: Mark 9:49

Neuter pan, everything (anything) whatsoever

a. in the singular: pan to followed by a participle 1 Corinthians 10:25, 27

b. Plural, all things

Used of a certain definite totality or sum of things, the context showing what things are meant: Mark 4:34

Accusative panta (adverbially), wholly, altogether, in all ways, in all things, in all respects: Acts 20:35

Panta, in an absolute sense, all things that exist, all created things: John 1:3

With the article

In an absolute sense, all things collectively, the totality of created things, the universe of things: Romans 11:36

In a relative sense: Mark 4:11

Panta ta followed by a participle Matthew 18:31

And ta panta with pronouns: ta ema panta, John 17:10

Panta hosa: Matthew 7:12

Panta with prepositions it forms adverbial

Pro pantoon, before or above all things

With negatives

not everyone

no one, none,

- **Theological Lexicon:**
  1. With Article
     a. pás can have different meanings according to its different uses.
     b. With the article it may have a predicative position with implicative ('all,' 'whole'),
     c. distributive ('whoever,' 'all possible'),
     d. elative significance ('all,' e.g., knowledge in 1 Corinthians 13:2)
     e. may have an attributive position ('whole,' 'generally'; cf. Acts 20:18).
  2. Without Article.
     a. may have elative ('full,' 'total')
     b. distributive significance ('each,' 'whoever,' 'whatever,'
     c. in privative phrases, 'any' ['without any'] or 'none,' 'nothing' ['not any').
  3. pás as Noun: With Article
     a. may have implicative ('all,' mostly plural) or summative ('in all,' 'all together') significance.
  4. Without Article.
     a. may have distributive significance ('each,' 'all'),
     b. may be used in adverbial phrases (e.g., 'first or last of all,' 'in every respect,' 'above all,' 'in all circumstances,' hence 'certainly').
  5. In Luke hápas is sometimes preferred when something impressive is to be said, especially with an implicative meaning and after a consonant, but in the main it is used in exactly the same way as pás.

The influence of Origen and his mentors / followers on the early church:

Consider this: A child is in need of a life-saving medical procedure. The parents receive a list of recommended professionals to perform the surgery. Two names top the list for consideration.

As a protective parent, one would do research on the credentials of the experts and would search and read the published papers regarding these professionals by their peers who are also highly trained and respected in this field. As a result of this research, the parents discover that behind one name, all the major doctors and medical institutions have placed their "seal" of approval and recommendation as a highly reliable source of help.

However, the second name has only a few positive references. In fact, the most respected institutions, have removed this doctor from their list of authorized practitioners. And, to make matters worse, the individuals who trained this "doctor" have themselves been removed from practice at these same institutions.

Question: to which one would you place the life of your child?

I propose that the same principles should be applied when selecting a source of expertise for development of doctrinal issues of salvation.

I have heard from my childhood, in the seed of inception are the roots of its destruction…

If some of the early scholars of Trinitarian Theology were rejected by the early church and its leadership, then a question should also be raised regarding all theology they held when they were rejected.

The lineage of Origen, an early proponent of the Trinitarian thought, shows a rejection by the church of those influencing, and influenced by, Origen.

- **Catholic Encyclopedia**

  According to Clement (Origen's mentor / teacher – rs) though Christ's goodness operated in the creation of the world, the Son himself was immutable, self-sufficient, and incapable of suffering… to Clement both the Son and the Spirit are 'first-born powers and first created'; they form the highest stages in the scale of intelligent being, and Clement distinguishes the Son-Logos from the Logos who is immutably immanent in God… to him, the body of Christ was not subject to human needs…

  Clement has had no notable influence on the course of theology beyond his personal influence on the young Origen.

- **Catholic Encyclopedia**

  Origen's cosmology is complicated and controverted, but he seems to have held to a hypothesis of the preexistence of souls. Before the known world was created by God, he created a great number of spiritual intelligences. At first devoted to the contemplation and love of their creator, almost all of these intelligences eventually grew bored of contemplating God, and their love for him cooled off. Those whose love for God diminished the most became *demons*. Those whose love diminished moderately became human souls, eventually to be incarnated in fleshly bodies. Those whose love diminished the least became *angels*. One, however, who remained perfectly devoted to God became, through love, one with the Word (*Logos*) of God. The Logos eventually took flesh and was born of the *Virgin Mary*, becoming the God-man *Jesus Christ*.

Origen studied under Clement. The doctrine of the resurrection of the body he upheld by the explanation that the Logos maintains the unity of man's existence by ever changing his body into new forms, thus preserving the unity and identity of personality in harmony with the tenet of an endless cosmic process. Origen's concept of the Logos allowed him to make no definite statement on the redemptive work of Jesus. Since sin was ultimately only negative as a lack of pure knowledge, the activity of Jesus was essentially example and instruction, and his human life was only incidental as contrasted with the immanent cosmic activity of the Logos. Origen regarded the death of Jesus as a sacrifice, paralleling it with other cases of self-sacrifice for the general good. On this, Origen's accord with the teachings of the Church was merely superficial.

If anyone does not anathematize *Arius*, *Eunomius*, *Macedonius*, *Apollinaris*, *Nestorius*, *Eutyches* and Origen, as well as their impious writings, as also all other heretics already condemned and anathematized by the Holy Catholic and Apostolic Church, and by the aforesaid four Holy Synods and [if anyone does not equally anathematize] all those who have held and hold or who in their impiety persist in holding to the end the same opinion as those heretics just mentioned: let him be anathema.

He represents a progressive purification of souls, until, cleansed of all clouds of evil, they should know the truth and God as the Son knew him, see God face to face, and attain a full possession of the Holy Spirit and union with God. The means of attainment of this end were described by Origen in different ways, the most important of which was his concept of a purifying fire which should cleanse the world of evil and thus lead to cosmic renovation. By a further spiritualization Origen could call God himself this consuming fire. In proportion as the souls were freed from sin and ignorance, the material world was to pass away, until, after endless eons, at the final end, God should be all in all, and the worlds and spirits should return to a knowledge of God; in Greek this is called *Apokatastasis*.

Eusebius stands entirely upon the shoulders of *Origen*. Like Origen, he started from the fundamental truth of the absolute sovereignty (monarchia) of God. God is the cause of all beings. But he is not merely a cause; in him everything good is included, from him all life originates, and he is the source of all virtue. God sent Christ into the world that it may partake of the blessings included in the essence of God. Christ is God and is a ray of the eternal light; but the figure of the ray is so limited by Eusebius that he expressly distinguishes the Son as distinct from Father as a ray is also distinct from its source the sun.

Eusebius was intent upon emphasizing the difference of the persons of the Trinity and maintaining the subordination of the Son (Logos, or Word) to God. The Logos, the Son (Jesus) is a hypostasis of God the Father whose generation, for Eusebius, took place before time. The Logos acts as the organ or instrument of God, the creator of life, the principle of every revelation of God, who in his absoluteness and transcendence is enthroned above and isolated from all the world. Eusebius, with most of the Christian tradition, assumed God was immutable. Therefore, to Eusebius's mind, the Logos must possess divinity by participation (and not originally like the Father), so that he can change, unlike God the Father. Thus he assumed a human body without altering the immutable divine Father. (Eusebius never calls Jesus o theós, but theós) because in all contrary attempts he suspected either polytheism (three distinct gods) or *Sabellianism* (three modes of one divine person).

Likewise, Eusebius described the relation of the Holy Spirit within the Trinity to that of the Son to the Father. No point of this doctrine is original with Eusebius, all is traceable to his teacher Origen. The lack of originality in his thinking shows itself in the fact that he never presented his thoughts in a system. After nearly being excommunicated due to charges of heresy by Alexander of Alexandria, Eusebius submitted and agreed to the *Nicene Creed* at the *First Council of Nicea* in 325. God has not made nature nor the substance of the soul bad; for he who is good can make nothing but what is good. Everything is good which is according to nature. Every rational soul has naturally a good free-will, formed for the choice of what is good.

Like many third-century Christian scholars, Arius was influenced by the writings of *Origen*, widely regarded as the first great theologian of Christianity. However, while he drew support from Origen's theories on the Logos, the two did not agree in all areas of doctrine. Arius clearly argued that the Logos had a beginning and that the Son, therefore, was not eternal. He also argued that the Son is clearly subordinate to the Father, the Logos being the highest of the Created Order. This idea is summarized in the statement 'there was a time when the Son was not (did not exist).

Macedonius on being ejected from Constantinople, bore his condemnation ill and became restless; he therefore associated himself with the other faction that had deposed Acacius and his party at Seleucia. By this means he drew around him a great number of adherents, who from him are still denominated Macedonians.

To this party Eustathius joined himself, who for the reasons before stated had been ejected from the church at Sebastia. But when Macedonius began to deny the Divinity of the

Holy Spirit in the Trinity, Eustathius said: 'I can neither admit that the Holy Spirit is God, nor can I dare affirm him to be a creature.'

... A discussion was then renewed on some of those points which they had previously determined and they no longer concealed but openly declared that the Son was altogether unlike the Father, not merely in relation to his essence, but even as it respected his will; asserting boldly also, as Arius had already done, that he was made of nothing. Being therefore questioned by them, how they dared to affirm that the Son is unlike the Father, and has his existence from nothing, after having acknowledged him God of God' in their former creed? They endeavored to elude this objection by such fallacious subterfuges as these. The expression, "God of God." said they, is to be understood in the same sense as the words of the apostle, but all things of God." Wherefore the Son is of God, as being one of these all things:

Consider this: You are made aware that a small drop of poison potent enough to cause death has been added to a five-gallon container of water . You have five other containers of water stored with the tainted water. You are not certain which bottle is the tainted container. What would you do?

I believe I would remove all potential containers holding the poison. I do not think I would take the chance my family, or myself, could be poisoned by the toxin and die. I would be overly cautious. Allow me to ask, should one not take the same care with a subject so important as salvation and eternity? Is it too much to place to the side those "scholars" that the majority of church leaders have consistently rejected?

My Response to Trinitarian Theology:

Before I close, allow me to share my belief about Trinitarianism. But, before I do, allow me a moment of clarification. Many times in scripture and in conversation, the speaker will use a parable, a story, or an allegory to simply express a deeper truth. The story is needed because the truth being expressed is so much deeper or dramatic that it becomes difficult to describe. All aspects of truth and its reality cannot be shown or described adequately with words alone. So, a story is used; a parable is given; or an allegory is made. This style of communication will be true as I share my position.

This chapter is the summation of my thoughts and my stance on Trinitarianism. I did not enter this process predetermined as to where I would end standing. My desire was to test the inductive system of theology of Dr. Hodge. What follows is the result of hundreds of hours of study as well as innumerable prayers for wisdom and guidance. As I say this, I do not wish to imply those who stand on an opposite side have not invested equal, and in many cases more, effort. I simply say, having done all to stand, I stand.

Thomas Talbott said: "Heresy is 'adherence to a religious opinion contrary to church dogma'. Because dogma varies among denominations, what is considered heresy by one denomination or congregation may be accepted as doctrine or opinion by another. In a socially free world, free moral agents may identify with whichever perspectives and positions, persons and communities, and traditions (or subtraditions) they find most intellectually, emotionally, and spiritually palatable. However, the results of their exercise of this operational freedom may be understood or interpreted differently by different persons."

I entered this study with an open mind. Like others, I want to know the truth as revealed in God's Word more than I want to stand where my mentors have stood. I also want to stand in the spirit of Francis Chan when he wrote in, Erasing Hell, "Let's be eager to leave what is familiar for what is true. Nothing outside of God and His truth should be sacred to us."

Chan further asks, "Do you want to believe in a God who shows His power by punishing non-Christians and who magnifies His mercy by blessing Christians forever?... Could you believe in a God who decides to punish people who don't believe in Jesus?... you may not recognize the difference immediately, but read them and you will see that these two questions – do you want to? versus, could you? – are actually miles apart.

"... It is important then to understand that Christian Universalists (hopeful and dogmatic) believe that salvation is by grace through faith in Christ and Christ alone. There's nothing untraditional about this. The difference is that they believe people will have another chance (or many chances) after death to believe in Jesus and be saved."

After investing much time in personal study of the verses and the comments of theologians from the past; having read and studied through resources like "Hyper-Grace", by Michael Brown; "Free Grace Soteriology" by David Anderson; "Erasing Hell", by Francis Chan; "This Son of Mine", by Malcolm Smith; "Love Wins", by Rob Bell, and "Hyper Grace Gospel", by Paul Ellis, I have come to the following conclusions:

- **First, all have sinned and come short of God's glory.**

King David of Israel said, "For I was born a sinner—yes, from the moment my mother conceived me." (Psalm 51:5) I am not a sinner because I sin - I sin because I'm a sinner.

The Apostle Paul takes it a step further when he says, "So the trouble is not with the law, for it is spiritual and good. The trouble is with me, for I am all too human, a slave to sin. 15 I don't really understand myself, for I want to do what is right, but I don't do it. Instead, I do what I hate. 16 But if I know that what I am doing is wrong, this shows that I agree that the law is good. 17 So I am not the one doing wrong; it is sin living in me that does it. 18 And I know that nothing good lives in me, that is, in my sinful nature. I want to do what is right, but I can't. 19 I want to do what is good, but I don't. I don't want to do what is wrong, but I do it anyway." Romans 7:14-17. (NLT)

Many Trinitarians believe the issue is between the law and grace – the need to rightly divide the Word of God between the Old and New Covenant. They further believe that everything prior to the cross is strictly Old Testament and that Grace is after the cross. But, King David and the Apostle Paul, (Old and New Covenant writers), have said that man is born in (as) a sin(ner).

It is true that those after the cross were born with their sins already paid for by Christ Jesus. But it is equally true that each man is born separated from God. The penalty for man's sins has been accomplished but the sins of mankind have not been forgiven. A criminal sentenced to 20 years of solitary confinement cannot say his crime has been forgiven. He can only say he has paid the penalty for his crime. The act of retribution (payment) does not accomplish forgiveness; it only accomplishes payment of penalty. So, Isaiah is correct when he wrote, "It's your sins that have cut you off from God. Because of your sins, he has turned away and will not listen anymore." (Isaiah 59:2)

In this scripture, Isaiah clearly reveals several things: first, it is man's sins that separate humanity from God; second, because of man's sins, God has turned away from humanity; and third, He will not listen anymore until the payment is made. Isaiah also says in the first verse of chapter 59 that God's arm is not weak nor are His ears too hard of hearing. He will save you.

I understand that Isaiah is writing under the Old Covenant. So, let's look to a New Covenant writer in the book of Hebrews (chapter 7, verses 23 through 25), "There were many priests under the old system, for death prevented them from remaining in office. 24 But because Jesus lives forever, his priesthood lasts forever. 25 Therefore he is able, once and forever, to save those who come to God through him. He lives forever to intercede with God on their behalf."

If I understand the writer correctly, Jesus saves those (once and forever) "who come to God through Him." Prior to coming to God through Christ, I am separated. Because of Jesus' priesthood established on the cross, He intercedes on our behalf. Allow me to ask, why do I need intercession unless I am separated?

I may be born with my sins paid for, but in my birth I am brought into the human family alienated (separated) from God. It is my sin that caused the separation, and because of my sin, God has turned away.

Allow me to share a drawing that is commonly used to depict this truth:

In the first drawing, humanity is separated from God because of man's sin. However, in the second drawing a bridge of access has been made available by Jesus on the cross. He has paid the price of death and separation from God (Romans 6:23; Isaiah 59:2). He has absorbed God's wrath and paid the penalty for our sin.

However, until we come to God by faith in what the death of Christ accomplished, we are still separated. It is not God who is separated from us. Rather it is we who are separated from Him.

- **Second, I believe the price humanity pays for sin is death:**

Paul wrote to the Christians at Rome and said, "For the wages of sin is death, but the free gift of God is eternal life through Christ Jesus our Lord." (6:23) These verses also support the position that all humanity will die: Genesis 2:17; 3:19; Isaiah 3:11; Ezekiel 18:4; Romans 5:12; 1 Corinthians 6:9-10; Galatians 3:10; 6:7-8; James 1:15 and Revelation 21:18, to list a few.

I also believe this death is both spiritual and physical, meaning, all of mankind will one day physically die. And, all of mankind is born spiritually dead. I want to be clear and say that even while man is physically alive, he is born spiritually dead.

Christ used this fact to answer a question posed to Him by a religious leader of the Jews – Nicodemus in John 3. It seems that this highly intelligent religious leader had questions about eternal subjects; specifically, how can humanity live with God in Heaven forever? It appears he was fearful of speaking with this radical Jewish teacher and so he came to Jesus at night.

After a quick compliment on the power of God at work in the miracles of Jesus, Nicodemus was startled when Jesus abruptly responded, "You won't see God's kingdom in Heaven unless you are born again."

This allegory used by Jesus caused Nicodemus to ask, "How can a man go back into his mother's womb and have a second birth?" While Jesus was speaking about a spiritual birth, this religious leader was interpreting the conversation as physical birth. Nicodemus was thinking of the birth process into Adam's family, while Jesus spoke of the birth process into God's family.

Trinitarians say they cannot believe or accept (follow) a god who would deal with humanity in anger; who would punish humanity in a literal place like hell. I was told by my Trinitarian friend that he totally rejects the concept found in the two drawings above. So, I asked him to draw for me his vision of that spiritual truth. I am including it below to help explain the difference of view between the two of us.

I apologize for the crudeness of the drawings, however, I am attempting to show to you, the reader, an accurate depiction of his thinking.

My friend began to explain. "In Adam, all of humanity die." For emphasis, he asked me, "How many die?" and he answered for me, "All!"

Then he stated, "In Christ, all are made alive." Again for clarity he asked, "How many are made alive? All!" he declared.

My friend explained he does not see a gulf (drawing one) between mankind and God. There is no need to cross the divide of our sin by faith (drawing two) in Christ's death, burial, and resurrection. Humanity's sins are gone; they no longer exist, because Christ paid for them on the cross (New Covenant). I was also told that, "Everyone is a child of God's – whether we know it or not!" (drawing three) I was assured that when Paul spoke on Mars' Hill, Paul was declaring all of humanity are under God and are one, and are His children, thus their "Unknown God." (Acts 17:23)

Acts 17:26, From one man he created all the nations throughout the whole earth. He decided beforehand when they should rise and fall, and he determined their boundaries. 27 His purpose was for the nations to seek after God and perhaps feel their way toward him and find him—though he is not far from any one of us. 28 For in him we live and move and exist. As some of your own poets have said, 'We are his offspring.'

Let me stop and paint a picture. I receive an invitation from one of my banks on a regular basis asking me to allow them to cancel all my debt. They assure me that I am pre-qualified. They entice me by saying they have placed more than enough finances in reserve to cover all my debts. The money is there; it is available; I meet the qualifications, there is just one thing keeping me from this wonderful opportunity… I have to exercise my will (faith and trust) and cash the check. Until I cash their check, even though the money is placed in reserve for me, it does me no good.

The difference between my Trinitarian friend and me is, we both realize the money (price of my debt) has already been set aside in an account – paid for by Jesus. However, I am not personally benefitted by this fact until I draft the checks and submit them to my accounts. That demands an act of faith on my part. I cannot claim my debts are paid and I am free of debt just because someone placed the money in an account bearing my name.

Using this story as a template for my friend would mean he sees himself, and all humanity, as not in debt. All the debts have been paid - for everyone. There is no need to cash a check as that would be an act of works and in his view it is a matter of grace. He would simply rest in this truth and send a "thank you" note for placing the money in his account.

There is a problem though. The holders of my debt are still waiting to be paid. I am separated from their good graces and when the debt is due, I would be found lacking. The law would be used against me and I would go to prison, (hell for the sake of my illustration), even though the banker had placed the money in my account. The money in the account means nothing unless I step forward and cash the check.

- **Third: I believe all sin and its consequences was paid for through the death, burial, and resurrection of God's Son, Jesus, by the shedding of His blood.**

When Jesus died on the cross He declared it was finished (John 19:30).

Here is what Adam Clarke's Commentary says about that declaration of Christ, ""I have executed the great designs of the Almighty-I have satisfied the demands of his justice - I have accomplished all that was written in the prophets, and suffered the utmost malice of my enemies; and now the way to the holy of holies is made manifest through my blood."

I could quote many other theologians, but the overwhelming majority of scholars identify these words on the cross as Christ's triumphant shout to the ages that all the Father requires, all that our sin demands, has been accomplished.

There are no more works or actions that can be added. What He has done is enough. Mankind looks to Him, and Him alone, for the passage into the Father's presence. One eternal breath of Heaven's air is because of Him. There is no more punishment required – it is finished.

Just as a side note, I am an advocate of the blood atonement as a requirement for God's salvation. Without the shedding of blood there is no remission of sin (Hebrews 9:22-28).

- **Fourth: I believe all sins and their consequences have been completely paid for, for every sinner, by Jesus' sacrifice on the cross.**

I fall between the Trinitarian and the Calvinist. One group believes all are already forgiven and will spend eternity in Heaven. The other holds that only a select group comprise the eternally forgiven inhabitant of Heaven: the chosen, just, forgiven, born again, saved, righteous, whatever term you desire.

Yes, I believe Jesus died for the sin of the whole world (1 John 2:2). I also believe Jesus is not willing that anyone would perish but that everyone would come to repentance (2 Peter 3:9). But, the reality of scripture would indicate to me that not everyone is - to use Jesus' word to Nicodemus - born again (Matthew 7:14; 22; Luke 16:23; Acts 26:28).

Jesus experienced separation from the Father, death, hell, rejection, and hanging on the cross to make payment for the penalties for every sin every human has ever (or will ever) commit. He is our High Priest. He is the only one to make intercession for mankind. He rose again the third day as proof of His victory. He ascended to the Father and has for the past 2,000 years been sitting at the Father's right hand making intercession for us.

He offers this gift of eternal life to everyone. However, unless each person personally "cashes the check" they will die in their sin. They will experience separation from God. They will be placed forever in the Lake of Fire which was prepared for the devil and his angels.

I cannot take those held truths and arrive at a destination that all are His child; all are forgiven. All sins are paid for – yes. But only the individual who, by faith, believes, are forgiven.

- **Fifth: I believe those who accept God's offer of grace and, by faith, receive His payment as their own, have inherited eternal life.**

The offer is to us individually. The offer is God's responsibility and the acceptance of that offer is our responsibility. It is not based on works of righteousness which we have done (Matthew 7:22, 23). There are no works that can be offered (James 2). It is God's grace and your faith coming together to "birth" you into God's family.

Paul told the Christians at Ephesus, "God saved you by his grace when you believed. And you can't take credit for this; it is a gift from God. Salvation is not a reward for the good things we have done, so none of us can boast about it." (2:8, 9).

It is first and foremost by God's grace or "unearned favor." It is the greater stooping down to the lesser and meeting a need only the greater could meet and the lesser does not deserve. His grace has been part of His character since eternity past. There is not an Old and New Covenant when it comes to God's grace.

The offer of what already exists does not do the individual any good until, "… when you believed."

You may be born with your sins already paid for and God's grace already moving in your direction. However, the personal benefit does not engage until YOU exercise your faith and believe.

It is totally of YOUR faith. I emphasize that because, as discussed earlier in this book, some Trinitarians believe it is the faith of Jesus that saves. It is not your own faith or that would be a work. Therefore, all you need to do is thank Him for His gift.

But, what can be learned from the following verses? They seem to clearly indicate it is your personal faith, working in conjunction with God's grace, that makes salvation personal.

Galatians 2:20, I am crucified with Christ: nevertheless I live; yet not I, but Christ liveth in me: and the life which I now live in the flesh I live by the faith of the Son of God, who loved me, and gave himself for me. (KJV)

Romans 1:17, This Good News tells us how God makes us right in his sight. This is accomplished from start to finish by faith. As the Scriptures say, "It is through faith that a righteous person has life." (NLT)

Romans 5:1, Therefore, since we have been made right in God's sight by faith, we have peace with God because of what Jesus Christ our Lord has done for us. 2 Because of our faith, Christ has brought us into this place of undeserved privilege where we now stand, and we confidently and joyfully look forward to sharing God's glory. (NLT)

Galatians 2:16, Yet we know that a person is made right with God by faith in Jesus Christ, not by obeying the law. And we have believed in Christ Jesus, so that we might be made right with God because of our faith in Christ, not because we have obeyed the law. For no one will ever be made right with God by obeying the law." (NLT)

Galatians 3:11, So it is clear that no one can be made right with God by trying to keep the law. For the Scriptures say, "It is through faith that a righteous person has life." (NLT)

- **Sixth: I believe those who remain, by choice, outside the grace of God at the time they enter eternity will spend eternity separated from God.**

    Philippians 1:28, Don't be intimidated in any way by your enemies. This will be a sign to them that they are going to be destroyed, but that you are going to be saved, even by God himself. 29 For you have been given not only the privilege of trusting in Christ but also the privilege of suffering for him. (NLT)

Paul's teaching seems to indicate there is a distinction in destination between the followers of Jesus and others. His followers will be blessed and we are privileged to suffer for Him in this world. However, the enemies of the Christian only look forward to destruction.

Paul continues in Philippians 3:19, by saying, "For I have told you often before, and I say it again with tears in my eyes, that there are many whose conduct shows they are really enemies of the cross of Christ. 19 They are headed for destruction. Their god is their appetite, they brag about shameful things, and they think only about this life here on earth." (NLT)

If I understand Paul's warning or encouragement, depending on the side you stand, these verses seem to clearly say that the enemies of the cross are headed for destruction.

And how can the Trinitarian reject "a god" who rejects unbelievers and places them outside of His kingdom? I wonder what Jesus means to teach when He said in Luke 13:22, "Someone asked him, 'Lord, will only a few be saved?' He replied, 24 'Work hard to enter the narrow door to God's Kingdom, for many will try to enter but will fail. 25 When the master of the house has locked the door, it will be too late. You will stand outside knocking and pleading, 'Lord, open the door for us!' But he will reply, 'I don't know you or where you come from.' 26 Then you will say, 'But we ate and drank with you, and you taught in our streets.' 27 And he will reply, 'I tell you, I don't know you or where you come from. Get away from me, all you who do evil.'" (NLT)

Those listening to Jesus teach understood His words to indicate some will be saved and others will not. They even grasped, with astonishment, that only a "few" will be saved. The answer given does not sound as if Jesus accepts the Trinitarian view. It sounds as if some will be accepted. But it also indicates that others, even after they have died, will come and plead for God to allow them to enter Heaven. His response will be, "Get away from me…"

There is no indication from Jesus' teaching that the door will always be open; that His ear will always be attentive to their cry; that there is another chance once eternity has come.

In Francis Chan's book, "Erasing Hell", he lists the writings of many 1st Century scholars and their description of Hell. Overwhelmingly they speak of it as a place of darkness, torments, fire, eternal, unquenchable punishments. Yet, he did not find any scholars who spoke of it as temporary; as if one could escape. In fact, there is not any indication in any scripture that would give hope that hell is temporary. No story or clear teaching shows that those who have entered have an escape path. In fact, a simple reading of Luke chapter 16 would indicate a great gulf is fixed so that those wanting to leave Hell cannot. Nor can anyone wishing to leave Heaven find a pathway to exit.

- **Seventh: I believe that separation will be experienced in a place called hell.**

  Please read Francis Chan's book, "Erasing Hell."

- **Eighth: I believe Hell is eternal and once entered, there is no escape (great gulf fixed between, so those who would transfer cannot). There is no further opportunity to be "saved."**

  It should only take one clear statement on this subject to settle the issue. However, allow me to present several scriptures. It is because of these, and many other verses, that I believe this eighth point.

Mark 9:43, If your hand causes you to sin, cut it off. It's better to enter eternal life with only one hand than to go into the unquenchable fires of hell with two hands. 45 If your foot causes you to sin, cut it off. It's better to enter eternal life with only one foot than to be thrown into hell with two feet. 47 And if your eye causes you to sin, gouge it out. It's better to enter the Kingdom of God with only one eye than to have two eyes and be thrown into hell, 48 'where the maggots never die and the fire never goes out.' (NLT)

Matthew 25:41, "Then the King will turn to those on the left and say, 'Away with you, you cursed ones, into the eternal fire prepared for the devil and his demons. (NLT)

Matthew 13:40, "Just as the weeds are sorted out and burned in the fire, so it will be at the end of the world. 41 The Son of Man will send his angels, and they will remove from his Kingdom everything that causes sin and all who do evil. 42 And the angels will throw them into the fiery furnace, where there will be weeping and gnashing of teeth. (NLT)

Matthew 13:49, That is the way it will be at the end of the world. The angels will come and separate the wicked people from the righteous, 50 throwing the wicked into the fiery furnace, where there will be weeping and gnashing of teeth. (NLT)

Matthew 25:46, "And they will go away into eternal punishment, but the righteous will go into eternal life." (NLT)

2 Thessalonians 1:7, He will come with his mighty angels, 8 in flaming fire, bringing judgment on those who don't know God and on those who refuse to obey the Good News of our Lord Jesus. 9 They will be punished with eternal destruction, forever separated from the Lord and from his glorious power. (NLT)

Revelation 14:9, Then a third angel followed them, shouting, "Anyone who worships the beast and his statue or who accepts his mark on the forehead or on the hand 10 must drink the wine of God's anger. It has been poured full strength into God's cup of wrath. And they will be tormented with fire and burning sulfur in the presence of the holy angels and the Lamb. 11 The smoke of their torment will rise forever and ever, and they will have no relief day or night, for they have worshiped the beast and his statue and have accepted the mark of his name." (NLT)

Revelation 20:11, And I saw a great white throne and the one sitting on it. The earth and sky fled from his presence, but they found no place to hide. 12 I saw the dead, both great and small, standing before God's throne. And the books were opened, including the Book of Life. And the dead were judged according to what they had done, as recorded in the books. 13 The sea gave up its dead, and death and the grave gave up their dead. And all were judged according to their deeds. 14 Then death and the grave were thrown into the lake of fire. This lake of fire is the second death. 15 And anyone whose name was not found recorded in the Book of Life was thrown into the lake of fire. (NLT)

Having done all to stand, here I stand.

Closing Thoughts

It is my prayer that this book is a help and perhaps a challenge to you. It was not written to serve as a text book. My style and approach have been for the purposes of someone like me, the common man.

Could I have shared more specific details? Yes. But only at the loss of my original intention.

I will close with a return to Mr. DeYoung's evaluation of, "Love Wins." Mr. DeYoung says, "Bad theology hurts real people. So of all the questions raised in the book, the most important question every reader must answer is this: is it true? Is 'Love Wins' true to the word of God? That's the issue. Open a Bible, pray to God, listen to the faithful Christians of the past 2000 years, and answer the question for yourself."

I echo his thoughts. Do you want to know where to stand on Trinitarianism, or any doctrine? Then you must develop a regular habit of finding your doctrinal truth through a systematic theological process. Open your Bible, pray to God, listen to the faithful Christians of the past 2000 years, and find an answer for yourself. God is faithful. The Holy Spirit has been sent to be your guide into truth. There is no indication in Scripture that God will reveal a new doctrinal truth regarding salvation in the last days. God never contradicts Himself or His Word. So any belief you are prompted to believe that is contrary to God's clear revealed truth in His Word – reject!

I have a file on my computer filled with quotes from many different sources and subjects. I searched key words that would indicate a simplistic style of communication. I am enclosing a few of them at this point for no particular purpose other than to direct your thoughts into realizing the value and importance of simplicity.

"Out of complexity find simplicity." – Tom Ranier

"If the what is unclear then the how is not even on the radar." – Tom Ranier

"Understanding always precedes commitment." – Tom Ranier

"If you want the necessary to stand out, get rid of the unnecessary." – Tom Ranier

"Most of the outstanding leaders I have worked with are neither tall nor especially handsome; they often are mediocre public speakers; they do not stand out in the crowd; they do not mesmerize an attending audience with their brilliance or eloquence. Rather, what distinguishes them is their clarity and persuasiveness of their ideas, the depth of their commitment, and their openness to continually learning more." – Peter Senge

"You can't hold people accountable for things that aren't clear. If you're unwilling to make decisions with limited information, you can't achieve clarity." – Andy Stanley

"Time and again, (Ben) Carson seemed to start a sentence and then, halfway through, head in an entirely different direction. The result was, too often, a word

salad." – *Washington Post comment on Dr. Ben Carson's speech at RNC 2016*

"I have come to the conviction that if you cannot translate your thoughts into uneducated language, then your thoughts were confused. Power to translate is the test of having really understood one's own meaning." – *CS Lewis*

About the Author

Ron Sears was reared in a pastor's home with the truth of God being prevalent. As a result, the things of God became common to him.

While in college Ron met and married his best friend, Marilyn. Together they have 3 children and 6 grandchildren.

God has used the realities of this life to show Ron the necessity of truth, faith, and relationship with the eternal. And he has become a student of God and His revealed truth - realizing the things of God are not common.

This book looks into a portion of our uncommon God. It is written for those who, like Ron, are the average learner with a passion to find truth.

www.ingramcontent.com/pod-product-compliance
Lightning Source LLC
Chambersburg PA
CBHW022122080426
42734CB00006B/218